AIR FRYER COOKBOOK UK

1500 Day Delicious, Quick & Easy Air Fryer Recipes for Beginners and Pros with Easy to Follow Steps

BY ROBERT JONES

Disclaimer and Terms of Use:

Effort has been made to ensure that the information in this book is accurate and complete, however, the author and the publisher do not warrant the accuracy of the information, text and graphics contained within the book due to the rapidly changing nature of science, research, known and unknown facts and internet. The Author and the publisher do not hold any responsibility for errors, omissions or contrary interpretation of the subject matter herein. This book is presented solely for motivational and informational purposes only.

TABLE OF CONTENTS

INTRODUCTION

Hi everyone who loves perusing food blogs for new kitchen devices and exciting recipes. There is a high chance that you have heard about air fryers and what they can offer. The air fryer has made its name in the current market and it has become the latest addition in most households. It has attracted many people with a promise of frying foods with just hot air. Since the appliance has existed for a while, you probably have heard about it and would like to have one in your kitchen. It's a great device that you can use to prepare chicken nuggets, French fries, and deep-fried starters like samosas with very little oil. In addition, you can use the gadget to reheat leftover foods like drumsticks, which often get soggy when heated in a microwave.

Not only does the air fryer cooks deep-fried dishes but also you can use them to bake and roast food items. It offers versatility and convenience in a single device and hence, eliminates having multiple cooking appliances in your kitchen.

Generally speaking, an air fryer is appealing because the manufacturer claims that the gadget can fry food ingredients with zero or little amount of oil and can even drain the excess fats during the cooking process. Unlike deep fryers that we already know for quite some time, the air fryer cooks food items by simply coating them with a thin layer of oil and circulating heated air around at high speeds with the aid of a strong fan. This in turn produces a delicious crispy layer that is associated with fried foods.

Apart from saving you calories, the air fryer is incredibly safe, surprisingly versatile and easy to use. Keep in mind that an air fryer may not always produce what you desire. For this reason, it's recommended that you first read the manual booklet or do some research before attempting to cook your desired meal. Air fryers come with varying settings and modes depending on the brand you choose. This means that making the same meal may call for different settings if cooking it with different brands of air fryers. Failure to adjust the settings can cause your food to burn, dry or produce unwanted results. Sometimes, some trials and errors may be required in order to understand how your appliance works.

WHAT TO EXPECT
FROM THIS BOOK

This book contains a lot of information about air fryers including cooking tips on how to prepare your delicious dishes. The book has more than seventy recipes with different types of food groups. The ingredients used in each recipe are readily available in your nearest stores but you can substitute with another if it's hard to find a certain ingredient. The result will be the same but just a little change of taste. This book caters for everyone, whether you are a carnivore or vegetarian. You will also find recipes that are kid-friendly and gluten-free. Since the appliance is safe to use, you can even teach your grown-up kids to reheat or prepare simple meals when busy at work.

The recipes in this cookbook are divided into different categories namely: desserts, snacks, side dishes and seafood. You will also come across recipes for breakfast, lunch/brunch, and dinner. All the recipes in this book are well structured in a certain order. For instance, every recipe has a title, prep time, cooking time, number of servings, a unique sample picture, ingredients, instructions, nutritional values as well as some cooking tips.

In general, this book will educate you more about the air fryer, how it functions, cooking tips and the benefits of using the appliance. You will also get to know the types of air fryers which is a very important factor when purchasing one for your kitchen. The book also contains details on what to do after purchasing an air fryer. If you have never used an air fryer before, this book should guide you on how to operate it and the things you can air fry. It will guide you on how to perform a test run to ascertain that your machine works properly. In addition, you will learn how to clean and maintain your appliance in order to ensure optimum use of it.

WHAT IS AN AIR FRYER?

An air fryer is a small convection oven that mimics deep-fried foods. It promises to deliver a crispy and crunchy exterior in foods without extra fats and calories associated with deep-frying. Air fryers are built differently depending on the size, brand and price tag. However, there are several components to expect such as the fan, heating element, perforated basket, drawer and control features, which are located at the front of the appliance.

Most models do not need oil for the machine to function, although tossing the food with a little amount of oil before cooking will improve the texture and flavour of the final product. While it's possible to eat air-fried food with zero added oil, the magic about this machine is that it only needs just a small amount. A teaspoon of vegetable oil contains about 40 calories. The little oil you add usually helps in browning and caramelization to produce crispy and crunchy results.

What can be cooked in an air fryer?

An air fryer can be used to cook almost anything that you would make in a deep fryer or oven. However, this machine is not suitable for high-moisture foods like cheese. In addition, when cooking breaded foods, make sure everything adheres properly to prevent breading from being blown away. Some of the foods you can cook in this machine include chicken wings, French fries, tofu, doughnuts, vegetables, and seafood.

Air fryers have multiple functions that you can use such as pressure cook, grill, air fry, bake, reheat, slow cook, yoghurt, sauté and steam. Simply switch between the cooking modes when preparing different meals.

Types of air fryers available

- **Pull-out drawer air fryer**: This type has a removable drawer that the user pulls out to place or take-out food. During the cooking process, the user shakes it a few times to ensure even cooking. It's best suited for cooking dishes like crumbled foods, meatballs, vegetables, chicken, fish, frozen foods and reheating leftovers.
- **Rotating basket type**: This one has a basket that rotates automatically along with other accessories that allow baking, grilling and roasting. It's best for cooking roasted veggies and roast meat.
- **Self-stirring type**: This type is modified to have a built-in paddle that automatically stirs food around the bowl. You can use it for baked veggies, crumbled chicken, battered fish and chips.
- **Benchtop oven type**: This type of machine can air-fry, bake, grill and roast. It's best for chicken tenders, chicken wings and chips.

HOW DOES THE AIR FRYER WORK?

An air fryer does not fry food but instead cooks things with dry hot air. The appliance comes with a basket that has tiny holes which allow the circulation of hot air from the bottom to the top. This enables your food to cook uniformly even when food is piled up. The compact nature of the air fryer allows the hot air to take less time to reach the food resulting in faster cooking times. However, in some cases, you will need to either shake or flip food items when halfway through the timer to ensure even crispness and browning. To complete this task, you will need to remove the drawer holding the basket and then turn your food. Note that some high-end models come with a timer feature that notifies you when to turn or flip the food.

In theory, the air fryer mimics the concept of deep frying whereby you get your food crispy very quickly. An air fryer usually functions just like a convection oven. You just need to set the temperature on your appliance and then place the food into the drawer. Air is heated by the heating element which is then rapidly circulated by a fan around the food. Since the food is raised and contained in a perforated basket, the hot air can reach all the surfaces of your food. The end result is crispy, crunchy and browned food with no oil or just a little amount of oil.

Here is how an air fryer works:

1. You put your food into the basket of your air fryer, which is usually removable for easier cleaning.
2. On the control panel, you set the temperature and cooking time called for in a recipe. In most cases, the temperature is normally set between 180 degrees Celsius to 200 degrees Celsius while the cooking time depends on the type of food item and the crispness desired.
3. The heating element inside the gadget heats up the air inside and a strong fan circulates the hot air around the food cooking it evenly and creates a crispy exterior.
4. Some models come with a built-in timer that automatically shuts off the appliance when cook time is done.
5. Remove your cooked food from the basket and serve.

Nonetheless, while you can nearly deep-fry anything you like, this isn't the same with air fryers. For instance, an air fryer may not work well with foods with high moisture content like cheese. This is because melted cheese will slide off and collect on the bottom of the machine. Some dishes like pasta and rice need to be rehydrated before consumption and hence, can't be cooked in an air fryer.

In addition, some delicate vegetables like leafy greens burn easily and thus are not suitable for air-frying. However, frozen vegetables work well since the moisture in the ice will help preserve them.

BENEFITS OF USING
AN AIR FRYER

Nowadays, many people have turned to air fryers as an alternative to making healthier meals. Below are the benefits of using an air fryer:

- ## Can help in managing your weight

Although deep-fried food items are delicious, they are loaded with a lot of calories and unhealthy. This can easily lead to weight gain due to intake of unhealthful oils. If you often crave for crispy and crunchy foods, consider the air-frying cooking method because little oil is used to achieve the desired results. While deep-frying calls for a generous amount of canola or vegetable oil, air-fried foods just require addition of about a tablespoon of oil when using the air fryer. Therefore, air-fried foods will significantly reduce the amount of oil and calories consumed.

- ## Lowers the risk of acrylamide formation

According to health experts, deep frying foods are known to contain high amounts of toxic acrylamide which is linked to heart-related diseases. Acrylamide is a carcinogenic substance that is formed when carbohydrates are exposed to high temperatures. Air frying your food can help reduce acrylamide formation compared to deep frying.

In addition, when vegetable oil is reused for deep frying, which is the case in most restaurants, it continuously produces harmful chemicals known as reactive oxygen species. The quality of the oil usually degrades and may as well destroy potential antioxidants found in food.

- ## Faster food preparations

This is one of the reasons for investing in an air fryer. Not only does the appliance saves your precious time but also it saves countertop space. Most air fryer models are about the size of a coffee maker and this makes them ideal for small kitchens. In addition, the appliance can even cook different types of food such as crispy spring rolls, chicken wings, and salmon with roasted tomatoes within half an hour or less. Some devices can also cook whole chicken within an hour.

- ## Easier to clean up

In general, air fryers are easy to clean and maintain in your kitchen. Most of the models come with removable parts that you can wash in the dishwasher. Although a dishwasher may not be an option, several parts of the appliance feature a non-stick coating on the surface that prevents residue from sticking.

- **They are safer in your kitchen**

As you may have known by now, the air fryer is safer to use compared to conventional methods of deep frying. The cooking chamber in an air fryer is closed and hence, there is very little risk of burning yourself with oil while cooking. In addition, using the air fryer means there won't be any burning-hot oil left off to cool on your kitchen counter after cooking.

AIR FRYER COOKING TIPS

Things to do before using your appliance for the first time

- After purchasing, make sure you remove the stickers attached to the exterior as well as all other packaging from the appliance.
- Place the air fryer on a heat-resistant surface and away from other objects. Doing so will help prevent damage by steam.
- Pull the drawer to remove the basket and then take out all plastic packaging. Separate the inner and outer baskets by pressing the basket release button.
- Clean the baskets thoroughly with a non-abrasive sponge or dishwasher. Use a damp cloth to wipe the interior and exterior of the basket. Dry your basket with a dry towel. Return the basket to the machine.

How to do a test run

It's recommended that you test your machine before cooking with it for the first time. Doing so will help you get to know how the controls work and also verify if the device is working properly. The following steps will guide you on how to do a test run;

1. Start by connecting the machine to the power plug. Ensure the appliance is empty. Preheat for a few minutes. Your device may have a preheat button if it's a multi-function air fryer. Other devices come with analogue systems and they're preheated manually. To preheat manually, set the timer to five minutes and heat at 204°C.
2. Once preheating is done, the machine will beep. Remove the basket and allow it to cool for about five minutes. Return the basket to the air fryer. Set your desired time and temperature time and then check if the gadget is functioning properly.
3. When the time is over, the appliance will shut off automatically and will continuously make a beep sound. Remove the basket from the appliance and then leave it to cool for about 10 to 30 minutes. Your air fryer should be ready to cook your favourite dishes.

Tips for your air fryer basket

1. Make sure that you only remove the appliance when cooking food and cleaning. Avoid removing it often.
2. The handle usually has a button protector that prevents you from pressing the release button accidentally. You will have to slide the guard knob forward to release the basket.
3. Refrain from pressing the release button when taking out the basket. If you do so when carrying the basket, it may fall and result in serious accidents.

4. When pressing the basket release button, ensure the basket is placed on a heat-resistant surface.

Tips when cooking

1. Don't overcrowd the basket. If you often cook for a large family or company, it's wise to go for a larger appliance that will cater for all your needs. Avoid overfilling the basket since the hot air may not reach all the surfaces of compacted food and this could lead to undercooking. Besides, the food can also burn if it touches the heating element.
2. Add water if cooking foods rich in fats. Fatty foods such as bacon and chicken wings release grease which collects at the bottom of the drawer. The grease is prone to smoking at high temperatures and can alter the taste of the food. To prevent this from occurring, it's advisable to add sufficient amounts of water into the drawer prior to cooking. The water stops the grease from smoking.
3. Shake and turn your food for even cooking and browning. Turn the food when halfway the cook time if you want a crispy and crunchy exterior.
4. Make use of aluminium foil when dealing with crumbled foods. When cooking sticky or crumbled foods, lay aluminium foil on the bottom of the basket. This will prevent the coating from being rubbed off when shaking and it also makes cleaning a lot easier. Don't cover the entire base of the basket with foil since you will want air to flow from underneath. In addition, make sure the foil doesn't cover food near the fan and the heating element.
5. Avoid using too much oil. Just brush or toss your food with one or two teaspoons of cooking oil. Not only does too much oil add fat content and calories, but also it can lead to smoking which eventually changes the taste of food. Smoking can also produce free radicals that are known to cause cell damage.
6. Refrain from using aerosol sprays. Aerosol oils have a high risk of breaking down the non-stick coating on components and this can cause the production of toxic fumes.

What to do after air-frying

1. Pull out the drawer and then transfer the basket onto a heat-resistant surface. Let your food cool a little before serving to avoid injuries or burns. If the food is too oily, use a clean cloth or paper towel to blot the excess oil.
2. Remove grease collected in the drawer but do not discard it. You can use juices from the drawer to spread atop the food or use it as a dipping sauce.
3. Once the food cools enough to handle, add your desired seasoning to enhance flavour.
4. If there are leftovers, transfer into an airtight container and store in your fridge right away. You can reheat leftovers in a microwave or an air fryer and make sure you reheat properly to minimize the risk of foodborne illnesses.
5. Always clean the appliance after using it. After cleaning, return all the components and switch the air fryer on for two or three minutes to dry everything.

Air fryer cleaning tips

In general, air fryers are easy to clean but some brands are easier to clean than others. Although an air fryer cooks food with little oil, it may produce fat that ends up on the bottom of the basket drawer. It can be a little bit tough to remove accumulated fat or oil when you put off clean-ups. If you smell odours from the appliance or notice smoke when cooking, it could be a sign that grease has accumulated on the heating element or drawer. It could also mean there are leftover food particles stuck in the basket holes. For these reasons, you should make an effort of cleaning the appliance after every use.

How to clean your machine

Most models come with dishwasher-safe parts to make things easier. Since most cookware has a non-stick coating, it's important to refrain from scratching that coating. You can do this by not using steel wool or any abrasives that can scratch the non-stick coating. Here are tips when it comes to cleaning your appliance:

1. Never delay cleaning. Don't allow food particles to sit for quite a long time or you will have a tough time cleaning. Once done with cooking, unplug the appliance, leave it to cool and then discard any accumulated oil in the drawer. If preparing dishes with a sticky sauce like marinated ribs, make sure you clean the drawer and basket while still warm since it will be a lot easier.
2. Wash all removable parts with warm soapy water. Feel free to use a cloth or soft sponge with no abrasives. In case there are residues stuck on any part, soak in water with dish detergent to loosen food particles.
3. Poke out any food particle stuck in the grate or basket with a toothpick or wooden skewer. Dry the parts separately.
4. Use a damp cloth immersed in soapy water to clean the interior of the air fryer. Wipe off food debris and grease from the heating element. Then dry and reassemble.
5. Use a damp sponge or cloth to wipe the machine's exterior and then dry.

How to get rid of lingering odours

If you notice a strong smell when cooking, it could be an odour lingering in your machine. You can solve this issue by soaking the drawer and basket in soapy water for about 30 to 60 minutes prior to cleaning. If the odour still persists, rub half of a lemon over the drawer and basket and leave it to sit for about half an hour before cleaning.

MEASUREMENT CONVERSIONS

US Dry Volume Measurements

1/16 teaspoon	Dash
1/8 teaspoon	Pinch
3 teaspoons	1 tablespoon
1/8 cup	2 tablespoons (1 standard coffee scoop)
1/4 cup	4 tablespoons
1/3 cup	5 tablespoons plus 1 teaspoon
1/2 cup	8 tablespoons
3/4 cup	12 tablespoons
1 cup	16 tablespoons
1 pound	16 ounces

US Liquid Volume Measurements

8 Fluid ounces	1 Cup
1 Pint	2 Cups (16 fluid ounces)
1 Quart	2 Pints (4 cups)
1 Gallon	4 Quarts (16 cups)

US to Metric Conversions

1/5 teaspoon	1 ml (ml stands for milliliter, one thousandth of a liter)
1 teaspoon	5 ml
1 tablespoon	15 ml
1 fluid oz.	30 ml
1/5 cup	50 ml
1 cup	240 ml
2 cups (1 pint)	470 ml
4 cups (1 quart)	.95 liter
4 quarts (1 gal)	3.8 liters
1 oz.	28 grams
1 pound	454 grams

Metric to US Conversions

1 milliliter	1/5 teaspoon
5 ml	1 teaspoon
15 ml	1 tablespoon
30 ml	1 fluid oz.
100 ml	3.4 fluid oz.
240 ml	1 cup
1 liter	34 fluid oz.
1 liter	4.2 cups
1 liter	2.1 pints
1 liter	1.06 quarts
1 liter	.26 gallon
1 gram	.035 ounce
100 grams	3.5 ounces
500 grams	1.10 pounds
1 kilogram	2.205 pounds
1 kilogram	35 oz.

Temperature Conversions

Fahrenheit	Celsius	Gas Mark
275° F	140° C	gas mark 1 - cool
300° F	150° C	gas mark 2
325° F	165° C	gas mark 3 - very moderate
350° F	180° C	gas mark 4 - moderate
375° F	190° C	gas mark 5
400° F	200° C	gas mark 6 - moderately hot
425° F	220° C	gas mark 7 - hot
450° F	230° C	gas mark 9
475° F	240° C	gas mark 10 - very hot

Abbreviations

Cooking Abbreviation(s)	Unit of Measurement
C, c	cup
g	gram
kg	kilogram
L, l	liter
lb	pound
mL, ml	milliliter
oz	ounce
pt	pint
t, tsp	teaspoon
T, TB, Tbl, Tbsp	tablespoon

AIR-FRIED APPLE FRITTERS

Preparation Time: 10 minutes | Cooking Time: 6 minutes | Servings: 12

Ingredients:

- Apples - 2
- All-purpose flour - 120g (1 cup)
- Sugar - 2 tablespoons
- Baking powder - 1 teaspoon
- Salt - ½ teaspoon
- Ground cinnamon - ½ teaspoon
- Ground nutmeg - ¼ teaspoon
- Milk - 80ml (⅓ cup)
- Butter, melted - 2 tablespoons
- Egg - 1
- Lemon juice - ½ teaspoon

For the glaze:

- Icing sugar - 50g (½ cup)
- Milk - 2 tablespoons
- Ground cinnamon - ½ teaspoon
- Salt - 1 pinch

Directions

1. Core the apple and dice them into small cubes. You can peel the apples if desired.
2. Mix the flour, sugar, baking powder, salt, ground cinnamon and ground nutmeg.
3. Combine the milk, melted butter, egg, and lemon juice in a different bowl.
4. Add the wet ingredients to the dry ingredients.
5. Toss in the apples and put the mixture into the fridge for 5 minutes.
6. Preheat the air fryer to 180°C (360°F).
7. Line the air fryer basket with parchment paper.
8. Drop the apple fritters into 2-tablespoon balls onto the basket.
9. Place the basket into the air fryer and cook for 6 to 7 minutes.
10. Meanwhile, whisk the glaze ingredients together.
11. Once done, take the apple fritters out and pour the glaze on top before serving.

Nutrition Value:

Calories: 100 | Fat: 3g | Saturates: 2g | Carbs: 18g | Sugars: 8g | Fibre: 1g | Protein: 2g | Salt: 0.02g

FLUFFY AIR-FRIED PANCAKES

Preparation Time: 5 minutes | Cooking Time: 36 minutes | Servings: 6

Ingredients:

- All-purpose flour - 180g (1 ½ cups)
- Baking powder - 1 ½ teaspoons
- Granulated sugar - 2-3 teaspoons
- Kosher salt - ¼ teaspoon
- Large egg - 1
- Buttermilk - 375ml (1 ½ cups)
- Unsalted butter, melted - 2 tablespoons

Instructions:

1. Whisk the flour, baking powder, sugar, and salt in a large mixing bowl.
2. Combine the egg, milk, and melted butter in a different bowl.
3. Form a well in the centre of the dry ingredients and pour the wet mixture into it. Gently stir until just combined; small lumps are okay.
4. While the batter is resting, take a 6-inch cake pan and spray it generously with oil.
5. Preheat the air fryer to 180°C (360°F).
6. Drop half a cup of pancake batter with a measuring cup into the cake pan. Gently spread the batter with a rubber spatula, making sure it covers the entire pan bottom.
7. Air fry until the pancake is golden brown on top, which usually takes 6 to 8 minutes. You don't need to flip it over.
8. Once done, take out the cooked pancake and keep it warm.
9. Repeat until all remaining batter is cooked.
10. Serve immediately.

Nutrition Value:

Calories: 193 | Fat: 5g | Saturates: 3g | Carbs: 29g | Sugars: 5g | Fibre: 1g | Protein: 6g | Salt: 0.3g

EASY BACON IN AIR FRYER

Preparation Time: 2 minutes | Cooking Time: 10 minutes | Servings: 3

Ingredients:

- Streaky bacon - 6 rashers

Instructions:

1. Put the bacon in a single layer in the air fryer basket. Make sure that the layers do not overlap each other.
2. Set the temperature to 200°C (400°F) and the timer for 10 minutes.
3. Remove the bacon after the set time elapses or until it turns brown and reaches desired crispiness.
4. Transfer the bacon to a kitchen paper-lined plate and serve.

Nutrition Value:

Calories: 74 | Fat: 6g | Saturates: 4g | Carbs: 2g | Sugars: 0g | Fibre: 0g | Protein: 6g | Salt: 0.88g

AIR FRYER BREAKFAST FRITTATA

Preparation Time: 5 minutes | Cooking Time: 16 minutes | Servings: 2

Ingredients:

- Eggs - 4
- Milk - 4 tablespoons
- Cheddar cheese, grated - 40g (⅓ cup)
- Feta, crumbled - 60g (½ cup)
- Tomato, chopped - 1
- Spinach, chopped - 4g (⅛ cup)
- Parsley and basil, chopped - 1 tablespoon
- Spring onion, chopped - 2
- Salt and pepper, to taste
- Olive oil - ½ teaspoon

Instructions:

1. In a large mixing bowl, beat the eggs and milk together.
2. Stir in all the other ingredients except the olive oil, and mix until well combined.
3. Preheat the air fryer to 180°C (360°F).
4. Take a round springform tin that fits comfortably into the air fryer basket and line it with non-stick baking paper. Lightly brush all sides with olive oil to prevent sticking.
5. Transfer the egg mixture to the tin.
6. Place the tin in the air fryer.
7. Set the timer for 16 minutes.
8. After 12 minutes, check if the frittata is ready since all air fryers vary.
9. Remove the pan once done.
10. Allow to cool for 5 minutes, then run a knife around the edges to loosen it from the tin.
11. Plate the frittata, cut it into slices, and serve.

Nutrition Value:

Calories: 307 | Fat: 22g | Saturates: 11g | Carbs: 7g | Sugars: 5g | Fibre: 1g | Protein: 21g | Salt: 0.54g

SAUSAGE CASSEROLE IN AIR FRYER

Preparation Time: 10 minutes | Cooking Time: 20 minutes | Servings: 6

Ingredients:

- Hash browns - 450g (1 pound)
- Ground breakfast sausage - 450g (1 pound)
- Green bell pepper, diced - 1
- Red bell pepper, diced - 1
- Yellow bell pepper, diced - 1
- Sweet onion, diced - 13g (¼ cup)
- Eggs - 4
- Salt and pepper, to taste

Instructions:

12. Line the basket of the air fryer with foil.
13. Place the hash browns on the bottom of the air fryer.
14. Top with uncooked ground sausage.
15. Evenly arrange the diced peppers and onions on top.
16. Set the temperature to 180°C (360°F) and the timer for 10 minutes.
17. If needed, open the air fryer and mix up the casserole.
18. Crack the eggs in a bowl and pour them over the top.
19. Cook for another 10 minutes, making sure the temperature remains the same.
20. Plate and serve with salt and pepper.

Nutrition Value:

Calories: 517 | Fat: 37g | Saturates: 10g | Carbs: 27g | Sugars: 4g | Fibre: 3g | Protein: 21g | Salt: 0g

BREAKFAST BURRITOS IN AIR FRYER

Preparation Time: 20 minutes | Cooking Time: 15 minutes | Servings: 6

Ingredients:

- Medium potato - 1
- Oil - 1 tablespoon
- Salt - 1 teaspoon, plus more to taste
- Pepper - ½ teaspoon, plus more to taste
- Breakfast sausage - 227g (½ pound)

- Flour tortillas - 6
- Eggs - 4
- Whole milk - 60ml (¼ cup)
- Cheddar cheese. shredded - 120g (1 cup)

Instructions:

1. Coat the chopped potatoes with oil, salt, and pepper.
2. Place the potatoes in one layer in the air fryer basket.
3. Cook for about 8 minutes.
4. After the set time elapses, remove the cooked potatoes from the basket and set them aside.
5. Cook the sausage in a non-stick pan over medium heat, breaking them into crumbles until well cooked.
6. Remove the sausage and set aside. Keep the grease in the pan.
7. In a bowl, whisk the eggs and milk. Add a little salt and pepper to taste.
8. Pour the egg and milk mixture into the hot pan with the sausage grease.
9. Scramble the eggs in the pan. Remove and set aside.
10. Combine the cooked potatoes, sausage, eggs, and cheddar cheese in a bowl.
11. Spread the mix evenly into the tortillas and wrap them up. Stick a toothpick in to keep them closed.
12. Spray oil onto the burritos and place them into the air fryer.
13. Set the temperature to 200°C (400°F) and the timer to 7 to 8 minutes.
14. Spray the burrito and flip it halfway through cooking.
15. Transfer the breakfast burritos to a plate and enjoy!

Nutrition Value:

Calories: 484 | Fat: 27g | Saturates: 10g | Carbs: 37g | Sugars: 3g | Fibre: 2g | Protein: 22g | Salt: 1.09g

AIR-FRIED BACON AND EGG CUPS

Preparation Time: 10 minutes | Cooking Time: 10 minutes | Servings: 6

Ingredients:

- Bacon slices - 3
- Large eggs - 6
- Diced bell pepper (optional)
- Salt and pepper (optional)

Instructions:

1. Cut the bacon strips in half.
2. Take a muffin tin that can comfortably fit in the air fryer basket. Wrap the bacon around the insides of the muffin tin into a cup shape.
3. Crack one egg inside each bacon-lined tin.
4. You can now top it off with diced peppers, salt and pepper.
5. Carefully put the muffin tin on the air fryer basket and close it.
6. Set the temperature to 160°C (320°F) and the timer for 10 minutes. If you like your eggs dippy, you can set the timer for 8 minutes.
7. Once the set time elapses and the eggs are cooked to your liking, remove the muffin tin.
8. Plate the baked egg cups and sprinkle with green onion or any toppings of choice.
9. Serve hot.

Nutrition Value:

Calories: 115 | Fat: 9g | Saturates: 3g | Carbs: 0g | Sugars: 0g | Fibre: 0g | Protein: 8g | Salt: 0.16g

CRISPY AIR-FRIED BREAKFAST POTATOES

Preparation Time: 10 minutes | Cooking Time: 20 minutes | Servings: 4

Ingredients:

- Russet potatoes - 3-4
- Olive oil - 2-3 tablespoons
- Salt - 1 teaspoon
- Garlic powder - 1 teaspoon
- Onion powder - ½ teaspoon
- Sweet paprika - ½ teaspoon
- Cooking spray

Instructions:

1. Peel the potatoes and dice them into 1-inch cubes.
2. In a large bowl, toss the potatoes with the olive oil and seasoning, making sure that they're evenly coated on all sides.
3. Spray the air fryer basket with oil to prevent potatoes from sticking.
4. Transfer the potatoes to the air fryer basket.
5. Set the temperature to 200°C (400°F) and the timer to 20 minutes.
6. Shake the basket at least once at the halfway mark.
7. Remove the potatoes once the set time elapses.
8. Plate and serve hot.

Nutrition Value:

Calories: 212 | Fat: 9g | Saturates: 1g | Carbs: 30g | Sugars: 1g | Fibre: 2g | Protein: 4g | Salt: 0.59g

AIR FRYER BLUEBERRY BREAD

Preparation Time: 5 minutes | Cooking Time: 30 minutes | Servings: 15

Ingredients:

- Milk - 250ml (1 cup)
- Bisquick - 360g (3 cups)
- Protein powder - 30g (¼ cup)
- Eggs - 3
- Frozen blueberries - 285g (1 ½ cups)

Instructions:

1. In a large mixing bowl, mix the Bisquick and protein powder.
2. Take another bowl, and whisk the milk and eggs together.
3. Slowly add the wet ingredients to the dry ingredients and beat until well combined.
4. Stir in the frozen blueberries. The mixture should be thick.
5. Transfer the mixture into a loaf pan that fits comfortably in the air fryer.
6. Place the loaf pan in the air fryer.
7. Set the temperature to 180°C (360°F) and the temperature to 30 minutes.
8. Remove the pan after the set time elapses.
9. Insert a toothpick to check to see if the bread is done. The toothpick should come out clean.
10. Serve hot.

Nutrition Value:

Calories: 212 | Fat: 9g | Saturates: 1g | Carbs: 30g | Sugars: 1g | Fibre: 2g | Protein: 4g | Salt: 0.59g

TOAD IN THE HOLE IN AIR FRYER

Preparation Time: 4 minutes | Cooking Time: 4 minutes | Servings: 2

Ingredients:

- Bread - 2 slices
- Butter - 2 teaspoons
- Eggs - 2
- Cheddar cheese, shredded - 2 tablespoons
- Salt and pepper, to taste

Instructions:

1. Set the temperature of the air fryer to 115°C (340°F).
2. Using the bottom of a measuring cup, press a 2-inch hole in the centre of a slice of bread.
3. Spread butter on both sides of the bread.
4. Crack an egg into the pressed hole in the bread.
5. Place the bread with the egg in the air fryer and cook for 6-7 minutes.
6. Check the egg for the desired level of doneness and add an additional 1 to 2 minutes of cooking time if necessary.
7. During the last 2 minutes of cooking, add shredded cheese over the bread and egg.
8. Once the cheese melts, remove your toad in a hole from the air fryer and serve hot.

Nutrition Value:

Calories: 209 | Fat: 12g | Saturates: 6g | Carbs: 14g | Sugars: 2g | Fibre: 1g | Protein: 11g | Salt: 0.3g

AIR FRYER CORNISH PASTIES

Preparation Time: 5 minutes | Cooking Time: 8 minutes | Servings: 3

Ingredients:

- Leftover instant pot beef stew - 250ml (1 cup)
- Air fryer pie crust - 500g (1 pound)
- Egg wash
- Mixed Herbs - 1 teaspoon
- Salt and pepper

Instructions:

1. Drain and place the leftover beef stew in a large bowl.
2. Season it well with the mixed herbs and some salt, and pepper.
3. Roll out the pasty. Place the bottom of the pasty maker over to stamp out three pastie circles. You might need to roll a second time to get three circles.
4. Place the cut-out pasty circles on a floured work surface.
5. Once you are done making the pasty circles, place them one at a time into the cutter.
6. Spoon some stew filling into one half of the circle.
7. Clamp the pasty cutter down to seal the pastie and create a beautiful pattern
8. Repeat until all the pasties are ready.
9. Line the air fryer basket with foil.
10. Place the pasties in a single layer in the foil-lined air fryer basket. You may need to work in batches.
11. Brush the tops of the cornish pasties with egg wash.
12. Set the temperature to 200°C (400°F) and the timer to 8 minutes.
13. Remove the cornish pasties once the set time elapses.
14. Plate and serve.

Nutrition Value:

Calories: 860 | Fat: 47g | Saturates: 6g | Carbs: 81g | Sugars: 1g | Fibre: 4g | Protein: 25g | Salt: 0.72g

SUNDAY PORK ROAST IN AIR FRYER

Preparation Time: 5 minutes | Cooking Time: 50 minutes | Servings: 6

Ingredients:

- Boneless roast pork leg or shoulder - 1.5kg (3.3 pounds)
- Olive Oil - 1 tablespoon
- Kosher Salt - 2 tablespoons

Instructions:

1. Take the pork out of its packaging and pat it dry with a paper towel.
2. Use a sharp knife to make shallow cuts on the rind at 1 cm intervals, being careful not to cut into the meat. You can also ask your butcher to do this step for you.
3. Sprinkle salt over the skin and rub it in.
4. Set aside the meat for at least 10 minutes to allow the salt to draw moisture from the rind and improve the crackling process.
5. Coat the pork with olive oil and generously sprinkle salt on the rind, rubbing it into the cuts.
6. Preheat the air fryer to 180°C (360°F).
7. Cook the roast for 50 minutes (25 minutes per pound of meat).
8. When the time elapses, check the internal temperature of the roast to ensure it has reached 60°C (140°F) in the thickest part.
9. Once done, transfer the roast to a carving board or plate.
10. Allow it to rest for 10 minutes before carving and serving.

Note: Cooking times depend on how big or thick the pork roast is. To ensure it's cooked all the way through, use a meat thermometer to check the inside temperature.

Nutrition Value:

Calories: 750 | Fat: 56g | Saturates: 20g | Carbs: 0g | Sugars: 0g | Fibre: 0g | Protein: 58g | Salt: 2.5g

BEST AIR FRYER HAMBURGERS

Preparation Time: 15 minutes | Cooking Time: 10 minutes | Servings: 4

Ingredients:

- Lean ground beef - 450g (1 pound)
- Worcestershire sauce - 1 tablespoon
- Salt - ½ teaspoon
- Pepper - ½ teaspoon
- Onions powder - ½ teaspoon
- Garlic powder - ½ teaspoon
- Barbecue sauce - 60ml (¼ cup)
- Hamburger buns - 4
- Lettuce, tomatoes, pickles, and onions, to serve

Instructions:

1. Prepare the air fryer by preheating it to 200°C (400°F).
2. In a large bowl, combine the ground beef, salt, pepper, onion powder, and garlic powder. Be gentle while mixing to get a soft texture and more flavour.
3. Shape the mixture into flour patties around a one-half inch thick each.
4. Use your thumb to make a slight indentation in the middle of the patty. Brush the patties with barbecue sauce.
5. Transfer the patties to the basket. Lay them out in a single layer.
6. Air fry the patties for 6 minutes.
7. Flip them over and cook for an additional 3 to 5 minutes.
8. If desired, you can top it off with cheese and cook for 1 more minute.
9. Once the burger is ready, serve it on buns with lettuce, tomatoes, pickles, and onion.

Nutrition Value:

Calories: 365 | Fat: 19g | Saturates: 7g | Carbs: 22g | Sugars: 3g | Fibre: 1g | Protein: 25g | Salt: 0.58g

CLASSIC ROAST BEEF IN AIR FRYER

Preparation Time: 5 minutes | Cooking Time: 35 minutes | Servings: 6

Ingredients:

- Beef roast - 900g (2 pounds)
- Olive oil - 1 tablespoon
- Medium onion - 1 (optional)
- Salt - 1 teaspoon
- Rosemary and thyme - 2 teaspoons

Instructions:

1. Start by preheating the air fryer to 200°C (400°F).
2. Take a plate and mix sea salt, rosemary and oil on it.
3. Pat the beef roast dry with paper towels and place it on the plate with the oil-herb mixture, turning it so that the outside is coated well.
4. If using, peel and cut an onion in two. Place the onion halves in the air fryer basket.
5. Transfer the beef roast to the air fryer basket.
6. Set the air fryer timer to 5 minutes.
7. After 5 minutes, increase the temperature to 180°C (360°F). Depending on your air fryer, you may need to flip the beef roast halfway through the cooking time.
8. Set the beef to cook for an additional 30 minutes for medium-rare. Use a meat thermometer to ensure it's cooked to your liking, and cook for additional 5-minute intervals if you want it more well done.
9. Once done, remove the roast beef from the air fryer, cover it with kitchen foil and let it rest for at least 10 minutes before serving. This will allow the meat to finish cooking and the juices to reabsorb into the meat.
10. Finally, carve the roast beef thinly against the grain and serve with roasted or steamed vegetables, wholegrain mustard, and gravy.

Nutrition Value:

Calories: 212 | Fat: 7g | Saturates: 2g | Carbs: 2g | Sugars: 1g | Fibre: 1g | Protein: 33g | Salt: 0.08g

SPRING ROLLS IN AIR FRYER

Preparation Time: 45 minutes | Cooking Time: 10 minutes | Servings: 8

Ingredients:

- Sesame oil - 2 tablespoons
- Minced garlic - ½ teaspoon
- Shredded cabbage - 180g (2 cups)
- Matchstick carrots - 128g (1 cup)
- Mushrooms - 88g (1 cup)
- Celery stalk - 1
- Fresh lime juice - 1 teaspoon
- Fish sauce -1 teaspoon
- Soy sauce - 1 teaspoon
- Corn starch -1 teaspoon
- Egg - 1
- Square spring roll wrappers - 8

Instructions:

1. Prepare the air fryer by preheating it to 200°C (400°F).
2. Heat the sesame oil in a skillet over medium heat and sauté the garlic for 30 seconds.
3. Add in all the vegetables and cook until they are tender.
4. Remove the skillet from the heat.
5. Stir the lime juice, fish sauce, and soy sauce into the vegetables.
6. Place the stuffing in each wrapper, just below the centre of the wrapper.
7. Roll up the wrapper halfway, tuck the sides in, and finish rolling.
8. Whisk the egg and add cornstarch into a thick paste.
9. Use the paste to seal the wrappers.
10. Place the spring rolls on the air fryer basket. You may need to work in batches.
11. Set the timer to 10 minutes.
12. After 5 minutes, turn it over.
13. Take out the spring rolls once the set time elapses and both sides are evenly brown.
14. Serve hot.

Nutrition Value:

Calories: 287 | Fat: 4g | Saturates: 1g | Carbs: 53g | Sugars: 2g | Fibre: 3g | Protein: 10g | Salt: 0.61g

HOMEMADE PIZZA IN AIR FRYER

Preparation Time: 5 minutes | Cooking Time: 7 minutes | Servings: 4

Ingredients:

- Mozzarella cheese, shredded - 40g (⅓ cup)
- Pizza dough - 12 inch
- Olive oil - 1 teaspoon
- Pizza sauce - 3 tablespoons
- Basil, freshly chopped - ¼ teaspoon

Instructions:

1. Prepare the air fryer by preheating it to 200°C (400°F).
2. Grease the air fryer basket with olive oil and line it with a parchment paper liner to stop the pizza from sticking.
3. Place the pizza dough on a clean, floured work surface.
4. Roll out the pizza dough to a size that fits comfortably in the air fryer basket.
5. Place it carefully on the air fryer.
6. Brush the top lightly with one teaspoon of olive oil.
7. Spread a light layer of pizza sauce and top it off with mozzarella cheese and any toppings of choice.
8. Set the temperature to 180°C (360°F) and the timer to 7 minutes.
9. Airy fry until the crust is crispy golden brown and the cheese has melted.
10. Remove the pizza from the air fryer.
11. Sprinkle it with basil, cheese, and red chilli flakes before serving.

Nutrition Value:

Calories: 58 | Fat: 3g | Saturates: 1g | Carbs: 4g | Sugars: 1g | Fibre: 1g | Protein: 3g | Salt: 0.17g

AIR FRYER GRILLED CHEESE SANDWICH

Preparation Time: 5 minutes | Cooking Time: 10 minutes | Servings: 1

Ingredients:

- Bread - 2 slices
- Butter - 1 tablespoon
- Swiss cheese (or any cheese that melts well) - 15g (⅛ cup)

Instructions:

1. Place cheese between the bread slices.
2. Spread butter on the outside of the bread.
3. Place the sandwich in the air fryer. Stick two toothpicks through the sandwich to hold them together securely.
4. Set the temperature to 180°C (360°F) and the timer to 10 minutes.
5. Flip the sandwich halfway through at 5 minutes.
6. Raise the heat to 200°C (400°F) and continue air frying for 5 more minutes. It is a good idea to watch the sandwich often to make sure that it doesn't burn.
7. Once done, remove the grilled cheese sandwich from the air fryer basket.
8. Enjoy the delicious grilled cheese sandwich as soon as it has cooled!

Nutrition Value:

Calories: 409 | Fat: 27g | Saturates: 15g | Carbs: 29g | Sugars: 4g | Fibre: 2g | Protein: 14g | Salt: 1.10g

TASTY AIR-FRIED SAUSAGE ROLLS

Preparation Time: 15 minutes | Cooking Time: 13 minutes | Servings: 20

Ingredients:

- Sausages - 6
- Ready rolled puff pastry - 320g (11 ounces)
- Semi-skimmed milk - 2 tablespoons
- Spray oil

Instructions:

1. Unroll the ready-rolled puff pastry.
2. Cut the roll into half lengthways to create two long thin strips.
3. Unwrap the sausages and arrange three along the middle of each pastry strip. You may need to squeeze them together to make them fit.
4. Brush one of the long edges of the pastry with some milk. Roll one long side of the pastry and seal tightly using a fork.
5. Using a sharp knife, cut the sausage rolls into length sizes that comfortably fit in your air fryer.
6. Make a few slight cuts on the top of each sausage roll.
7. Spray the basket of the air fryer with oil.
8. Arrange the sausage rolls in the basket so that they aren't touching. Depending on the size of your air fryer, you may need to cook them in batches.
9. Brush each sausage roll with some more milk.
10. Set the temperature to 200°C (400°F) and the timer for 13 minutes.
11. Check the sausage rolls halfway through to ensure that they are not burning.
12. Once the set time elapses, the sausage rolls should be crisp and golden brown on the outside and steaming hot on the inside.
13. Transfer the sausage rolls to a plate and cool for a few minutes before serving.

Nutrition Value:

Calories: 124 | Fat: 5g | Saturates: 2g | Carbs: 1g | Sugars: 1g | Fibre: 1g | Protein: 3g | Salt: 0.13g

AIR-FRIED PIZZA POCKETS

Preparation Time: 15 minutes | Cooking Time: 15 minutes | Servings: 4

Ingredients:

- Ready-to-bake puff pastry - 2 sheets
- Pizza sauce - 250ml (1 cup)
- Mozzarella cheese, shredded - 120g (1 cup)
- Pepperoni slices - 100g (¾ cup)

Instructions:

1. Allow the pastry sheets to thaw on the counter for approximately 10 minutes.
2. Lightly flour your work surface and lay the pastry sheets flat on the floured surface.
3. Divide the pastry sheets into four squares, making eight total pieces.
4. Spread pizza sauce over four squares and top it with shredded mozzarella cheese and pepperoni slices.
5. Put the four remaining pastry squares over the filling. Seal in the edges, enclosing the filling to form a parcel.
6. Arrange the pizza pockets in the air fryer.
7. Set the temperature to 180°C (360°F) and the timer for 15 minutes.
8. Once the set time elapses, put it on a plate and let it cool for a few minutes before serving.

Nutrition Value:

Calories: 459 | Fat: 34g | Saturates: 15g | Carbs: 14g | Sugars: 4g | Fibre: 1g | Protein: 23g | Salt: 1.29g

AIR-FRIED HAM, EGG, AND CHEESE SLIDERS

Preparation Time: 10 minutes | Cooking Time: 5 minutes | Servings: 6

Ingredients:

- Eggs - 3
- Hawaiian bread rolls - 6
- Swiss cheese - 6 slices
- Ham - 6 slices
- Butter melted - 4 tablespoons

- Brown sugar - 1 tablespoon
- Mustard - 1 tablespoon
- Salt and pepper, to taste
- Olive oil spray

Instructions:

1. In a bowl, whisk the eggs with some salt and pepper until the mixture becomes frothy.
2. Spray a Pyrex dish with cooking spray and pour the egg mixture into it.
3. Place the dish in the microwave and cook for 2 minutes. If the eggs are not cooked enough, microwave them for an additional minute.
4. Cut rolls in half horizontally, creating two separate top and bottom pieces.
5. Lay the bottom pieces of the rolls in a single layer on a clean surface.
6. Place a layer of ham on top of the roll bottoms, followed by a layer of cheese.
7. Once the eggs are ready, remove them from the microwave and place them on top of the ham and cheese layers on the rolls.
8. Cover the sandwiches with the remaining halves of the rolls.
9. Mix butter, brown sugar, and mustard in a small bowl. Microwave it for 20 seconds to melt the butter.
10. Pour the butter mixture over the sandwiches.
11. Preheat the air fryer to 175°C (350°F).
12. Place the sandwiches in a Pyrex dish and put it on the bottom rack of the air fryer.
13. Cook for 2 minutes.
14. Move the rack to the middle position and continue cooking until the sandwiches are heated, and the tops are golden brown.

Nutrition Value:

Calories: 378 | Fat: 14g | Saturates: 2g | Carbs: 17g | Sugars: 6g | Fibre: 1g | Protein: 19g | Salt: 0.72g

APPETISERS

AIR FRYER FISH CAKES

Preparation Time: 15 minutes | Cooking Time: 10 minutes | Servings: 4

Ingredients:

- Cod fillets, or any white fish, coarsely chopped - 340g (12 ounces)
- Bread crumbs - 100g (⅔ cup)
- Fresh cilantro, finely chopped - 2 tablespoons
- Sweet chilli sauce - 2 tablespoons
- Mayonnaise - 2 tablespoons
- Egg - 1
- Salt - ¼ teaspoon
- Black pepper powder- ¼ teaspoon
- Lemon wedges - 4

Instructions:

1. Prepare the air fryer by preheating it to 200°C (400°F).
2. Line the basket of the air fryer with parchment paper to prevent sticking.
3. Crush the chopped fish in a food processor until it is crumbly. If a food processor is unavailable, you can chop it manually to a fine mince.
4. Combine the crumbled fish, bread crumbs, cilantro, chilli sauce, mayonnaise, egg, salt, and pepper.
5. Carefully shape the fish cake mixture into four patties, about 2.5 cm.
6. Line the patties in a single layer on the air fryer basket.
7. Spray them with cooking oil.
8. Cook the fish cakes for 5 minutes.
9. Flip them over and spray them with cooking oil.
10. Cook them again for 4 to 5 more minutes. Once done, the cakes should be golden brown and crispy.
11. Remove from the air fryer.
12. Serve hot with lemon wedges.

Nutrition Value:

Calories: 176 | Fat: 8g | Saturates: 2g | Carbs: 4g | Sugars: 4g | Fibre: 1g | Protein: 20g | Salt: 0.42g

POTATO SCONES IN AIR FRYER

Preparation Time: 20 minutes | Cooking Time: 18 minutes | Servings: 4

Ingredients:

- All-purpose flour - 120g (1 cup)
- Baking powder - ½ tablespoon
- Salt - ½ teaspoon
- Butter - 1 ½ tbsp
- Potatoes, mashed in butter and milk - 125g (½ cup)
- Milk - 3 tablespoons
- Egg - 1 large

Instructions:

1. In a large bowl, blend the flour, baking powder, and salt.
2. Slice the butter into small cubes and toss it to the flour mixture. Blend the butter into the flour until the mixture resembles small pea-sized chunks.
3. In a separate mixing bowl, blend the mashed potatoes with the milk and eggs.
4. Combine the wet and dry ingredients and mix to create a crumbly dough.
5. Knead the dough until it becomes soft. If the dough is too sticky, add a small amount of flour and knead until it is no longer sticky.
6. Shape the dough into a long roll, then divide it into four equal parts. Roll each section out into a circle about 1 inch thick.
7. Place the scones on the air fryer basket in a single layer.
8. Set the temperature to 200°C (400°F) and the timer for 18 minutes.
9. Turn the scones over halfway through to ensure all sides are golden brown and crispy.
10. Once done, plate and serve warm with maple syrup or butter and jam.

Nutrition Value:

Calories: 199 | Fat: 6g | Saturates: 3g | Carbs: 30g | Sugars: 1g | Fibre: 1g | Protein: 6g | Salt: 0.51g

AIR-FRIED CRISPY PEPPER RINGS

Preparation Time: 15 minutes | Cooking Time: 9 minutes | Servings: 4

Ingredients:

- Large bell peppers - 2
- All-purpose flour - 40g (⅓ cup)
- Salt - ½ teaspoon
- Eggs - 2

For breading:

- Panko bread crumbs - 100g (⅔ cup)
- Seasoned bread crumbs - 50g (⅓ cup)
- Olive oil - 2 teaspoons

Instructions:

1. Crack the eggs in a small bowl and whisk them with the salt.
2. Mix the Panko bread crumbs, seasoned bread crumbs, and olive oil in a small bowl and combine well.
3. Cut the bell peppers into one-half inch rings and season well with salt. Toss with flour.
4. Dip the pepper rings into the egg mixture first. Next, dip it into the breading mixture. Make sure that the rings are coated evenly on all sides.
5. Preheat the air fryer to 200°C (400°F).
6. Arrange the coated peppers in a single layer in the air fryer basket. If your air fryer basket is small, you may need to cook them in batches.
7. Air fry for 9 minutes or until golden brown.
8. Serve hot with dipping sauce.

Nutrition Value:

Calories: 183 | Fat: 5g | Saturates: 1g | Carbs: 26g | Sugars: 4g | Fibre: 2g | Protein: 7g | Salt: 0.53g

AIR-FRIED MOZZARELLA STICKS

Preparation Time: 15 minutes | Cooking Time: 8 minutes | Servings: 4

Ingredients:

- Mozzarella cheese sticks - 8
- Egg - 1
- Milk - 2 tablespoons
- Italian seasoning - 1 teaspoon
- Panko bread crumbs - 75g (½ cup)
- Seasoned bread crumbs - 75g (½ cup)

Instructions:

1. Unwrap the mozzarella cheese sticks.
2. Place the cheese on a parchment-lined plate and put it in the freezer for 30 minutes.
3. While the cheese is freezing, beat the egg and milk in a bowl.
4. In a separate bowl, mix the bread crumbs and the Italian seasoning.
5. Dip the frozen mozzarella cheese sticks in the egg mixture, then roll them in the breadcrumb mixture.
6. Put the coated cheese sticks in a single layer on the air fryer basket.
7. Set the temperature to 200°C (400°F) and the timer to 8 minutes.
8. Once the mozzarella sticks are golden brown and crispy, serve them warm with your favourite dipping sauce.

Nutrition Value:

Calories: 161 | Fat: 8g | Saturates: 4g | Carbs: 13g | Sugars: 1g | Fibre: 1g | Protein: 10g | Salt: 0.64g

QUICK NACHOS IN AIR FRYER

Preparation Time: 4 minutes | Cooking Time: 4 minutes | Servings: 4

Ingredients:

- Tortilla chips - 104g (4 cups)
- Cheese, shredded - 240g (2 cups)
- Green onion - 1
- Black olives - 45g (¼ cup)
- Tomatoes, diced - 100g (½ cup)
- Jalapenos, chopped - 26g (¼ cup)
- Cilantro, chopped - 2 tablespoons
- Sour cream or guacamole, to serve

Instructions:

1. Preheat the air fryer to 160°C (320°F).
2. Spread a single layer of tortilla chips on the air fryer basket or tray.
3. Sprinkle shredded cheese, black olives, diced onions, and diced jalapenos on top of the chips.
4. Place the basket or tray in the preheated air fryer and cook for 3 to 5 minutes or until the cheese is melted and the chips are crispy.
5. Remove the nachos from the air fryer and top them with diced tomatoes and chopped cilantro.
6. Serve immediately with sour cream or guacamole.

Note: Cooking time may vary depending on the air fryer model and the number of nachos. Keep an eye on them while they are cooking and adjust the time accordingly.

Nutrition Value:

Calories: 527 | Fat: 34g | Saturates: 14g | Carbs: 40g | Sugars: 2g | Fibre: 4g | Protein: 19g | Salt: 0.73g

AIR-FRIED EGGPLANT BITES

Preparation Time: 10 minutes | Cooking Time: 12 minutes | Servings: 4

Ingredients:

- Large eggplant - 1
- Bread crumbs - 100g (⅔ cup)
- Parmesan cheese, grated - 2 tablespoons
- Italian seasoning - 1 teaspoon
- Garlic powder - ¼ teaspoon
- Eggs - 2
- All-purpose flour - 30g (¼ cup)
- Marinara sauce, to serve (optional)

Instructions:

7. Slice the eggplant to make circles about ⅓ inch thin.
8. Sprinkle the eggplant slices with salt and let them sit for 20 minutes.
9. While the eggplant is sitting, mix the bread crumbs, grated parmesan cheese, Italian seasoning, and garlic powder in a medium-sized bowl.
10. In a separate bowl, beat the eggs with one tablespoon of water.
11. Give the eggplants a quick rinse and pat dry.
12. Dip the eggplant slices into the flour to coat them on both sides. Next, dip it into the egg and then into the breadcrumb mixture. Spray oil on both sides of the eggplant.
13. Set the temperature to 200°C (400°F) and the timer to 12 minutes.
14. Arrange the eggplants in a single layer in the air fryer basket.
15. Flip the eggplants over halfway through.
16. Remove from the air fryer once the set time elapses and the eggplant bites are golden brown, tender and crisp.
17. Dip into warm marinara sauce and enjoy.

Nutrition Value:

Calories: 171 | Fat: 4g | Saturates: 1g | Carbs: 26g | Sugars: 5g | Fibre: 5g | Protein: 8g | Salt: 0.21g

AIR-FRIED STUFFED JALAPENOS

Preparation Time: 5 minutes | Cooking Time: 7 minutes | Servings: 2

Ingredients:

- Jalapenos - 3
- Cream cheese - 44g (¼ cup)
- Nacho cheese mix, shredded - 30g (¼ cup)
- Bacon bits - 1 tablespoon
- Green onion - 1

Instructions:

1. Prepare the air fryer by preheating it to 180°C (360°F).
2. Slice the jalapenos lengthwise into two halves and remove all the seeds.
3. Put the cream cheese, nacho cheese mix, bacon bits, and sliced green onion in a small bowl and mix until well combined.
4. Stuff each jalapeno with the cheese mixture.
5. Place the stuffed jalapenos in a single layer on the air fryer basket.
6. Air fry the peppers for about 7 minutes until the jalapenos are tender and the cheese on top is a brilliant brown.
7. Serve immediately as an appetiser.

Nutrition Value:

Calories: 171 | Fat: 4g | Saturates: 1g | Carbs: 26g | Sugars: 5g | Fibre: 5g | Protein: 8g | Salt: 0.21g

HOT WINGS IN AIR FRYER

Preparation Time: 5 minutes | Cooking Time: 24 minutes | Servings: 2

Ingredients:

- Chicken wings - 450g (1 pound)
- Olive oil - 1 tablespoon
- Salt and pepper, to taste
- Hot sauce - 125ml (½ cup)

Instructions:

1. Spritz the basket of the air fryer with cooking spray and set aside.
2. Prepare the chicken wings by patting them dry and sprinkling them with salt and pepper.
3. Arrange the chicken wings in the air fryer basket in a single layer, making sure they are not touching each other. You may need to line up the drumettes upright along the sides to fit them. You might also need to cook them in batches, depending on the size of your air fryer.
4. Set the temperature to 180°C (360°F).
5. Air fry the wings for 12 minutes. Flip them over using tongs and cook for another 12 minutes.
6. Flip the wings once again. Raise the temperature to 200°C (400°F) and cook for about 6 minutes more until the outsides are crisp.
7. Toss the wings in hot sauce to coat them thoroughly.
8. Put them back in the air fryer basket and cook for 2 minutes.
9. Plate and serve hot.

Nutrition Value:

Calories: 340 | Fat: 27g | Saturates: 6g | Carbs: 1g | Sugars: 1g | Fibre: 1g | Protein: 23g | Salt: 1.68g

AIR FRYER STEAK BITES

Preparation Time: 5 minutes | Cooking Time: 15 minutes | Servings: 12

Ingredients:

- Sirloin steak or strip loin or ribeye - 450g (1 pound)
- Vegetable oil - 1 tablespoon
- Soy sauce - 1 tablespoon
- Worcestershire sauce - 1 ½ teaspoons
- Garlic cloves - 2
- Salted butter - 1 tablespoon
- Salt and pepper, to taste
- Fresh parsley - 1 tablespoon

For Horseradish Dipping Sauce:

- Sour cream - 60g (¼ cup)
- Mayonnaise - 2 tablespoons
- Prepared horseradish - 1 ½ tablespoons
- Fresh lemon juice - 1 teaspoon
- Garlic clove - 1
- Salt and pepper, to taste

Instructions:

1. Cut the steak into small bite-size pieces, about 1 inch in size.
2. Season with oil, soy sauce, Worcestershire sauce, garlic, salt, and pepper.
3. Allow the mixture to marinate for 15 minutes.
4. Preheat the air fryer to 200°C (400°F)
5. After removing the steak bites from the marinade, pat them dry and then toss them in melted butter.
6. Place the steak bites in the air fryer basket, making sure they are not overcrowded and have space to cook evenly.
7. Cook the steak bites for 6 to 7 minutes or until they reach your desired level of doneness.
8. Once cooked, remove the steak bites from the air fryer and let them rest for a few minutes.
9. Whisk together the ingredients for horseradish dipping sauce.
10. Toss with fresh parsley and serve with horseradish sauce.

Nutrition Value:

Calories: 215 | Fat: 11g | Saturates: 4g | Carbs: 1g | Sugars: 1g | Fibre: 1g | Protein: 25g | Salt: 0.36g

AIR-FRIED PICKLE CHIPS

Preparation Time: 20 minutes | Cooking Time: 9 minutes | Servings: 4

Ingredients:

- Dill pickle slices - 215g (1 ½ cups)
- All-purpose flour - 30g (⅓ cup)

- Eggs - 2
- Seasoned salt - ½ teaspoon

For breading:

- Panko bread crumbs - 100g (⅔ cup)
- Seasoned bread crumbs - 50g (⅓ cup)

- Dried dill - 1 teaspoon
- Olive oil - 2 teaspoons

Instructions:

1. Whisk eggs and seasoned salt together in a small bowl (or freezer bag).
2. In a different bowl, combine the bread crumbs, dill, and oil.
3. Dab the pickles dry with paper towels and toss with flour.
4. Dip the floured pickles into the beaten egg mixture, and remove, allowing the excess to drip off.
5. Next, dip them into the breading mixture, gently pressing to adhere.
6. Preheat the air fryer to 200°C (400°F).
7. Place pickles in a single layer in the basket of the air fryer.
8. Air fry for 7 to 9 minutes or until golden.
9. Repeat steps 4 to 8 with the remaining pickles.
10. Serve immediately.

Nutrition Value:

Calories: 172 | Fat: 5g | Saturates: 1g | Carbs: 24g | Sugars: 2g | Fibre: 2g | Protein: 7g | Salt: 0.99g

DINNER

CLASSIC SHEPHERD'S PIE IN AIR FRYER

Preparation Time: 20 minutes | Cooking Time: 20 minutes | Servings: 4

Ingredients:

- Sunflower oil - 1 tablespoon
- Onion, finely chopped - 1 large
- Carrots, chopped - 2 medium
- Minced beef - 500g (1 pound)
- Tomato purée - 2 tablespoons
- Worcestershire sauce - a large splash
- Beef stock - 500ml (2 cups)
- Medium potatoes - 3
- Butter - 185g (¾ cup)
- Milk - 3 tablespoons
- Cheese, shredded (optional)

Instructions:

1. Poke the potatoes with a fork and place them in the air fryer.
2. Bake the potatoes at 200°C (400°F) for 40 to 45 minutes until tender.
3. Take the potatoes out of the air fryer and scoop out the flesh.
4. Place the potatoes in a bowl and mash with the butter and milk until fluffy.
5. In a large skillet, sauté the chopped onions and carrots for a few minutes.
6. Crumble in the beef mince with the onion and carrots and cook until well browned.
7. Add the tomato purée and a generous splash of Worcestershire sauce and mix well.
8. Pour the beef stock in and bring the broth to a simmer until thickened, for 8-10 minutes.
9. Preheat the air fryer to 180°C (360°F).
10. Transfer the beef mixture into an air fryer-safe pan and spread the mash on top with a fork. Sprinkle cheese on top if desired.
11. Place the pan on the air fryer basket and cook for 10-15 minutes.

Nutrition Value:

Calories: 601 | Fat: 37g | Saturates: 17g | Carbs: 40g | Sugars: 3g | Fibre: 4g | Protein: 29g | Salt: 0.31g

TURKEY CROQUETTES IN AIR FRYER

Preparation Time: 20 minutes | Cooking Time: 10 minutes | Servings: 6

Ingredients:

- Potatoes, mashed in butter and milk - 500g (2 cups)
- Parmesan cheese, grated - 45g (1/2 cup)
- Swiss cheese, shredded - 60g (1/2 cup)
- Fresh rosemary, minced - 2 teaspoons
- Fresh sage, minced - 1 teaspoon
- Salt - 1/2 teaspoon
- Pepper - 1/4 teaspoon
- Cooked turkey, finely chopped - 420g (3 cups)
- Large egg - 1
- Water - 2 tablespoons
- Panko bread crumbs - 185g (1 ¼ cups)
- Cooking spray
- Sour cream, to serve

Instructions:

1. Preheat the air fryer to 180°C (360°F).
2. Combine the mashed potatoes, cheese, rosemary, sage, salt and pepper in a bowl.
3. Stir in the finely chopped turkey. Be gentle while mixing it, but ensure that it is blended thoroughly.
4. Shape the mixture into twelve 1-inch thick patties.
5. In a shallow bowl, beat the egg and water. Keep the bread crumbs in another shallow bowl.
6. Dip the patties into the egg mixture, then dip in the bread crumbs to coat thoroughly.
7. Arrange the croquettes in a single layer on a greased tray in the air fryer.
8. Spray with cooking oil.
9. Cook the croquettes for 4 to 5 minutes until golden brown.
10. Flip them over with tongs and spray them with cooking oil.
11. Cook for 4 to 5 more minutes, until all sides are golden brown.
12. Remove the croquettes from the air fryer.
13. Serve hot with sour cream.

Nutrition Value:

Calories: 322 | Fat: 12g | Saturates: 6g | Carbs: 22g | Sugars: 2g | Fibre: 2g | Protein: 29g | Salt: 0.67g

STUFFED PEPPERS IN AIR FRYER

Preparation Time: 25 minutes | Cooking Time: 12 minutes | Servings: 4

Ingredients:

- Bell peppers - 4
- Lean ground beef - 450g (16 ounces)
- Cooked rice - 140g (1 cup)
- Olive oil - 1 tablespoon
- Tomato sauce - 500ml (2 cups)
- Onion, chopped - ½
- Minced garlic - ½ tablespoon
- Salt and pepper, to taste
- Italian seasoning - 1 teaspoon
- Shredded mozzarella - 62g (¾ cup)

Instructions:

1. Cut off the tops of the bell peppers and scoop out the insides.
2. Cook the rice according to the package instructions.
3. Coat the peppers with olive oil using a brush, inside and out.
4. Place the oil-coated peppers into the air fryer.
5. Set the air fryer temperature to 150°C (300°F) and the timer for 5 minutes.
6. While the peppers are cooking in the air fryer, season the beef with salt and pepper.
7. In a medium saucepan, sauté the beef along with chopped onions and garlic over medium heat. The beef should be cooked until there is no more pink.
8. Drain the grease from the beef.
9. Add the cooked rice, tomato sauce, and Italian seasoning to the beef and simmer for 4 minutes.
10. Stuff the beef mixture into the peppers.
11. Place the stuffed peppers back into the air fryer.
12. Cook at 180°C (360°F) for 8 minutes.
13. Open the air fryer, top the peppers with shredded mozzarella and place back into the air fryer for another 3 to 4 minutes.
14. Remove the peppers once the set time elapses or once the tops are golden brown.
15. Serve hot.

Nutrition Value:

Calories: 460 | Fat: 21g | Saturates: 8g | Carbs: 28g | Sugars: 8g | Fibre: 4g | Protein: 40g | Salt: 0.87g

AIR-FRIED CHICKEN THIGHS

Preparation Time: 5 minutes | Cooking Time: 45 minutes | Servings: 4

Ingredients:

- Small chicken thighs with skin on - 8
- Olive oil - 1 tablespoon
- All-purpose flour - 1 tablespoon
- Seasoning of choice (Salt and pepper, or smoky BBQ, garlic granules, celery salt, or ras-el-hanout)

Instructions:

1. Rub each chicken thigh in the olive oil so that they are well-coated.
2. In a small bowl, combine the flour with your seasoning of choice.
3. Toss in the chicken thighs, ensuring that all sides receive a generous coating.
4. Lay out the chicken in a single layer on the air fryer basket.
5. Set the temperature to 180°C (360°F) and the timer for 35 mins.
6. Once the set time elapses, pull off the flesh on the underside from one piece to check if the chicken is well-cooked. It should come away with ease, and no pink should remain. The skin should be crispy. If needed, cook for a few more minutes.
7. Immediately remove the chicken from the fryer to a dish. Leaving it in the airy fryer will cause the steam to make the skin soft again.
8. Lay aside for at least 5 minutes. Waiting allows the chicken to reabsorb the juices instead of dripping onto your plate.

Nutrition Value:

Calories: 250 | Fat: 16g | Saturates: 4g | Carbs: 4g | Sugars: 0g | Fibre: 0.6g | Protein: 22g | Salt: 0.24g

AIR FRYER BAKED POTATOES

Preparation Time: 2 minutes | Cooking Time: 50 minutes | Servings: 4

Ingredients:

- Large-sized baking potatoes - 4
- Olive oil - ½ tablespoon
- Sea salt - ½ teaspoon
- Garlic Powder - ½ teaspoon
- Toppings of choice (can be butter, cheese, baked beans, or tuna mayonnaise)

Instructions:

1. Wash the potatoes, dry them well with kitchen paper, and transfer them to a plate.
2. Drizzle oil over the potato and rub it into the skins using your hands so that all sides of the potatoes are well-coated.
3. Generously sprinkle them with sea salt and garlic powder. Use your hands to spread everything around to make sure that it has an even coat.
4. Place the potatoes in one layer in the air fryer basket.
5. Set the temperature to 200°C (400°F) and the timer for 50 mins.
6. Use tongs to rotate the potatoes if they are browning too quickly on top.
7. Remove the potatoes after the set time elapses or until a fork pierces through the potatoes easily. Once done, the potato skin should be crispy, and the inside should be soft and fluffy.
8. Split the potato in half and serve immediately with butter, cheese, baked beans, tuna mayonnaise, or any topping of your choice.

Nutrition Value:

Calories: 206 | Fat: 2g | Saturates: 0.4g | Carbs: 40g | Sugars: 3g | Fibre: 5g | Protein: 5g | Salt: 0.01g

HONEY GARLIC PORK CHOPS IN AIR FRYER

Preparation Time: 10 minutes | Cooking Time: 15 minutes | Servings: 4

Ingredients:

- Pork chops - 4
- Salt and pepper for seasoning
- Honey - 4 tablespoons
- Garlic cloves, minced - 2
- Lemon juice - 2 tablespoons
- Sweet chilli sauce - 1 tablespoon
- Extra virgin olive oil - 1 tablespoon

Instructions:

1. Preheat the air fryer to 200°C (400°F).
2. Coat all sides of the pork chops thoroughly with salt and pepper.
3. Arrange the pork chops in a single layer in the air fryer basket, making sure they lay flat on the bottom.
4. Cook for 15 minutes, flipping halfway through. You may need to cook longer if the pork chops are thicker.
5. While the pork chops are cooking, put the sauce together. In a small pan, heat olive oil over medium heat and sauté the garlic until it turns golden brown. It usually takes 30 seconds to a minute.
6. Add the lemon juice, sweet chilli sauce, and honey to the pan and stir until well combined.
7. Simmer the sauce for 3 to 4 minutes on low heat until thickened. To make the sauce thicker, mix one tablespoon of cornstarch with one tablespoon of water in a small bowl and stir it in.
8. Once done, transfer the pork chops to a plate and drizzle the sauce over the top before serving.

Nutrition Value:

Calories: 435 | Fat: 21g | Saturates: 6g | Carbs: 21g | Sugars: 20g | Fibre: 0g | Protein: 40g | Salt: 0.16g

TIMELESS MEATLOAF IN AIR FRYER

Preparation Time: 10 minutes | Cooking Time: 35 minutes | Servings: 4

Ingredients:

For the loaf:

- Lean ground beef - 1 kg (2 pounds)
- Large eggs - 2
- Milk - 60ml (¼ cup)

- Bread crumbs - 100g (⅔ cup)
- Meatloaf seasoning - 3 tablespoons
- Worcestershire sauce - 1 tablespoon

For the topping:

- Ketchup - 250ml (1 cup)
- Light brown sugar - 55g (½ cup)

- Dijon mustard - 1 tablespoon
- Worcestershire sauce - ½ tablespoon

Instructions:

1. Take a large bowl and combine the beef, eggs, milk, bread crumbs, meatloaf seasoning, and Worcestershire sauce.
2. Knead and mix the ingredients thoroughly using your hands or a big spoon.
3. Transfer the mixture to a loaf pan to form it onto a loaf shape.
4. Turn the pan upside down and place the meatloaf in the air fryer.
5. Preheat the air fryer to 120°C (250°F).
6. Set the timer for 25 minutes and cook it.
7. Meanwhile, combine all the topping ingredients in a small bowl.
8. After the set time elapses, coat the meatloaf top with 4 tablespoons of the topping mixture.
9. Place the meatloaf in the air fryer again and cook for 5 to 10 minutes.
10. Remove the meatloaf from the air fryer.
11. Spoon additional topping mixture onto the meatloaf before serving.

Nutrition Value:

Calories: 189 | Fat: 9g | Saturates: 3g | Carbs: 13g | Sugars: 2g | Fibre: 1g | Protein: 14g | Salt: 0.45g

VEGAN FAJITAS IN AIR FRYER

Preparation Time: 10 minutes | Cooking Time: 15 minutes | Servings: 2-3

Ingredients:

- Portobello mushrooms - 4
- Sweet peppers - 2
- Large onion - 1
- Tortillas - 8

- Toppings of choice (can be guacamole, salsa, sour cream or vegan crema, chopped coriander)

For Fajita Sauce:

- Sweet chilli sauce - 3 tablespoons
- Soy sauce - 1 tablespoon
- Smoked paprika - 1 teaspoon

- Chilli powder - ⅛ teaspoon
- Cumin - ½ teaspoon
- Ground coriander - ¼ teaspoon

Instructions:

1. In a large mixing bowl, whisk the fajita sauce ingredients together.
2. Slice the mushrooms, peppers and onions into thin strips.
3. Toss the striped vegetable into a large bowl and combine it with the fajita sauce.
4. Set the temperature to 200°C (400°F).
5. Stir the spice-coated vegetables with a drizzle of oil.
6. Transfer the vegetables to the air fryer basket.
7. Allow the vegetables to cook for 15 minutes, stirring the vegetables halfway through.
8. The fajita is ready when the vegetables are soft and a little crispy around the edges.
9. Serve hot with warmed tortillas and any toppings you choose.

Nutrition Value:

Calories: 720 | Fat: 19g | Saturates: 6g | Carbs: 121g | Sugars: 2g | Fibre: 12g | Protein: 21g | Salt: 1.45g

ITALIAN SAUSAGE IN AIR FRYER

Preparation Time: 5 minutes | Cooking Time: 27 minutes | Servings: 4

Ingredients:

- Oil - 1 tablespoon
- Sweet pepper - 1
- Small onion - 1
- Italian sausage links - 4
- Sausage rolls - 4

Instructions:

1. Remove the stem, seeds, and membranes from the sweet pepper. Then, slice it into thin strips.
2. Trim the top and bottom ends of the onion and peel off the outside layer. Next, slice the onion in half and cut both halves into long slices.
3. Take a non-stick pan that fits comfortably into the air fryer.
4. Place the pan in the air fryer.
5. Heat one tablespoon of oil in the pan at 160°C (320°F) in the air fryer for 1 minute.
6. Toss the sliced peppers and onions into the pan and cook for 10 to 12 minutes. Stir occasionally to cook evenly.
7. Remove peppers and onions from the air fryer.
8. Increase the temperature to 200°C (400°F) and cook the Italian sausage links for 10 to 12 minutes. Rotate the sausages halfway through so all sides are evenly cooked.
9. Remove the sausages from the air fryer.
10. Cut the sausage rolls down the middle about ¾ of the way down.
11. Stuff the sausage rolls with sausage links, peppers, and onions.
12. Place the rolls back in the air fryer at 200°C (400°F) degrees and cook for 1 to 2 minutes. The sausage roll should be crisp once done.
13. Serve hot.

Nutrition Value:

Calories: 623 | Fat: 47g | Saturates: 13g | Carbs: 26g | Sugars: 4g | Fibre: 1g | Protein: 23g | Salt: 1g

CHICKEN LEGS IN AIR FRYER BASKET

Preparation Time: 5 minutes | Cooking Time: 22 minutes | Servings: 6

Ingredients:

- Chicken drumsticks - 6
- Olive oil - 1 tablespoon
- Salt - 1 teaspoon
- Pepper - 1 teaspoon
- Garlic powder - 1 teaspoon
- Paprika - 1 teaspoon
- Onion powder - 1 teaspoon

Instructions:

1. Combine the olive oil and desired seasoning in a mixing bowl.
2. Add the chicken drumsticks to the bowl and toss to coat evenly.
3. Transfer the coated drumsticks to the basket and place the basket in the air fryer.
4. Set the air fryer temperature to 190°C (375°F) and the timer for 22 minutes.
5. Cook the chicken until the set time elapses or until the internal temperature of the meat reaches 75°C (165°F).
6. Turn off the air fryer and leave the basket to cool for a few minutes before serving.

Nutrition Value:

Calories: 209 | Fat: 16g | Saturates: 4g | Carbs: 1g | Sugars: 1g | Fibre: 1g | Protein: 14g | Salt: 0.46g

SEAFOOD

AIR-FRIED LOBSTER TAILS

Preparation Time: 10 minutes | Cooking Time: 10 minutes | Servings: 2

Ingredients:

- Lobster tails - 2
- Butter - 4 tablespoons
- Lemon zest - 1 teaspoon
- Garlic, grated - 1 clove

- Salt - 1 teaspoon
- Black pepper powder - 1 teaspoon
- Fresh parsley, chopped - 1 teaspoon
- Lemon wedges - 2

Instructions:

1. Prepare the air fryer by preheating it to 195°C (380°F).
2. Using a pair of kitchen shears, butterfly lobster tails by cutting through the middle of the hard top shells and meat. Cut the shells to the bottom, but not through it.
3. Spread the tail halves apart and place them in the air fryer basket with the lobster meat facing up.
4. Melt the butter in a small non-stick pan over low heat.
5. Sauté the lemon zest and garlic in the heated oil until the garlic is fragrant and light brown, which usually takes only about 30 seconds.
6. Spoon two tablespoons of the butter mixture into a small bowl. Brush the lobster tails with this mixture.
7. Season the lobster by sprinkling them with salt and pepper.
8. Air fry the seasoned lobsters in the preheated air fryer for 5 to 7 minutes until the lobster meat is opaque.
9. Once done, take the lobster out from the air fryer.
10. Spoon the leftover butter from the pan over the lobster meat. Top it off with parsley and serve immediately with lemon wedges.

Nutrition Value:

Calories: 313 | Fat: 26g | Saturates: 16g | Carbs: 3g | Sugars: 0g | Fibre: 1g | Protein: 18g | Salt: 0.59g

AIR FRYER CRAB CAKES

Preparation Time: 10 minutes | Cooking Time: 10 minutes | Servings: 4

Ingredients:

- Lump crab - 230g (8 ounces)
- Green onion, chopped - 2
- Red bell pepper, chopped - 38g (1/4 cup)
- Mayonnaise - 2 tablespoons
- Bread crumbs - 2 tablespoons
- Dijon mustard - 1 tablespoon
- Old bay seasoning - 1 teaspoon
- Oil for spraying
- Lemon wedges - 4

Instructions:

1. In a large bowl, mix the lump crab, green onion, red bell pepper, mayonnaise, bread crumbs, Dijon mustard, and old bay seasoning. Stir until well combined.
2. Shape the mixture into flour patties around 3/4 inch thick each.
3. Place the patties in the air fryer basket in a single layer, making sure they are not touching each other.
4. Lightly spritz the patty tops with oil.
5. Set the temperature to 195°C (380°F) and the timer to 10 minutes.
6. After cooking for 5 minutes, gently flip the crab cakes over.
7. Cook for the remaining 5 minutes until both sides are crispy brown.
8. Once the set time elapses, open the air fryer and take out the crab cakes.
9. Plate and serve with lemon wedges.

Nutrition Value:

Calories: 123 | Fat: 6g | Saturates: 1g | Carbs: 5g | Sugars: 1g | Fibre: 1g | Protein: 12g | Salt: 0.6g

BREADED OYSTERS IN AIR FRYER

Preparation Time: 10 minutes | Cooking Time: 10 minutes | Servings: 2

Ingredients:

- Oysters - 450g (1 pound)
- All-purpose flour - 60g (½ cup)
- Kosher salt - ½ teaspoon
- Black pepper powder - ¼ teaspoon
- Cajun seasoning - 1 teaspoon

- Large egg - 1
- Milk - 1 tablespoon
- Panko bread crumbs - 221g (1 ½ cups)
- Lemon wedges - 2
- Melted garlic butter, to serve

Instructions:

1. Prepare the air fryer by preheating it to 180°C (350°F).
2. Clean the oysters by scrubbing the outside of each shell with a stiff brush under cold running water.
3. Carefully shuck the oysters by inserting an oyster knife into the hinge of the oyster and twisting to pry it open.
4. Rinse the oysters under cold water and pat dry with a paper towel.
5. In a bowl, mix the flour, salt, pepper, and cajun seasoning.
6. In a separate bowl, whisk the egg and milk.
7. Put the panko bread crumbs in a third bowl.
8. Sprinkle the oysters with the flour mixture, dip them in the egg mixture, and finally roll them in the bread crumbs.
9. Place the oysters in the air fryer, making sure not to overcrowd the basket.
10. Spray lightly with cooking spray.
11. Air fry the oysters for 4 minutes.
12. Turn them over using tongs. Spray again lightly with cooking oil, and cook for 4 more minutes.
13. Carefully remove the oysters from the air fryer and serve immediately with lemon wedges and melted garlic butter.

Nutrition Value:

Calories: 123 | Fat: 6g | Saturates: 1g | Carbs: 5g | Sugars: 1g | Fibre: 1g | Protein: 12g | Salt: 0.6g

AIR FRYER SALMON

Preparation Time: 5 minutes | Cooking Time: 10 minutes | Servings: 4

Ingredients:

- Salt - 1 teaspoon
- Pepper - 1 teaspoon
- Mixed herbs - 1 teaspoon
- Garlic granules - 1 teaspoon (optional)
- Salmon fillets, with or without skin - 4 x 130g fillets
- Olive oil- ½ tablespoon
- Cooked seasonal greens, to serve (optional)
- Quinoa or brown rice, to serve (optional)

Instructions:

1. Mix the salt, pepper, mixed herbs, and garlic granules together in a large bowl.
2. Rub a little olive oil on each salmon fillet and roll in the seasoning to coat on all sides.
3. Place the salmon in the air fryer basket or tray in a single layer.
4. Set the temperature to 180°C (360°F) and the timer for 10 minutes.
5. Serve hot with seasonal greens and quinoa or brown rice as desired.

Nutrition Value:

Calories: 264 | Fat: 17g | Saturates: 3g | Carbs: 0.1g | Sugars: 0g | Fibre: 0.1g | Protein: 27g | Salt: 1.36g

AIR-FRIED CRISPY POPCORN SHRIMP

Preparation Time: 10 minutes | Cooking Time: 8 minutes | Servings: 4

Ingredients:

- All-purpose flour - 60g (½ cup)
- Eggs - 2
- Water - 2 tablespoons
- Panko bread crumbs - 221g (1 ½ cup)
- Ground cumin - 1 tablespoon
- Garlic powder - 1 tablespoon
- Shrimp, peeled and deveined - 450g (1 pound)
- No-salt-added ketchup - 125ml (½ cup)
- Chipotle chiles in adobo sauce - 2 tablespoons
- Fresh cilantro, chopped - 2 tablespoons
- Lime juice - 2 tablespoons
- Kosher salt - ⅛ teaspoon

Instructions:

1. Spray the air fryer basket with cooking oil to avoid sticking.
2. Place the flour in a shallow bowl.
3. Beat the eggs and water in another shallow bowl.
4. Mix the panko bread crumbs, ground cumin and garlic powder in a third shallow bowl.
5. Dip the shrimp in the flour, then in the egg, then in the bread crumbs.
6. Transfer the shrimp to the air fryer basket in a single layer. You may need to work in batches if the air fryer basket cannot hold all the shrimp.
7. Spray them generously with cooking oil.
8. Set the temperature at 180°C (360°F).
9. Cook the shrimp for 4 minutes and flip them over. Continue cooking for about 4 minutes until they are crisp and cooked through.
10. Repeat until all remaining shrimp are cooked.
11. Mix the ketchup, chipotles, chopped cilantro, lime juice and kosher salt in a small bowl.
12. Serve popcorn shrimp hot with the dipping sauce.

Nutrition Value:

Calories: 297 | Fat: 4g | Saturates: 1g | Carbs: 35g | Sugars: 9g | Fibre: 1g | Protein: 29g | Salt: 0.29g

GOLDEN AIR-FRIED SCALLOPS

Preparation Time: 10 minutes | Cooking Time: 6 minutes | Servings: 4

Ingredients:

- Scallops - 450g (1 pound)
- Olive oil - 1 teaspoon
- Cajun seasoning - 1 teaspoon
- Kosher salt, to taste

Instructions:

1. Preheat the air fryer to 200°C (400°F).
2. Rinse, then pat the scallops dry with a paper towel.
3. Spray the scallops with cooking oil and season with kosher salt and cajun seasoning until they are coated completely.
4. Line the preheated air fryer basket with aluminium foil and lightly grease it with cooking oil.
5. Arrange the seasoned scallops in a single layer on the air fryer basket, working in batches if needed.
6. Cook all the scallops in the air fryer for 3 minutes.
7. Flip the scallops over using tongs and cook for an additional 3 minutes until they are opaque. If the scallops are cooked all the way through, their temperature should register at a minimum of 55°C (130°F) internally.
8. Plate and serve hot with pasta, salad or roasted vegetables.

Nutrition Value:

Calories: 111 | Fat: 4g | Saturates: 1g | Carbs: 4g | Sugars: 1g | Fibre: 1g | Protein: 14g | Salt: 0.45g

AIR FRYER CRUNCHY CALAMARI

Preparation Time: 5 minutes | Cooking Time: 7 minutes | Servings: 4

Ingredients:

- Calamari rings - 450g (1 pound)
- Lemon juice - 3 tablespoons
- All-purpose flour - 60g (½ cup)
- Garlic powder - 1 teaspoon
- Egg whites - 2
- Milk - ¼ cup
- Panko bread crumbs - 295g (2 cups)
- Kosher salt - 1 ½ teaspoons
- Black pepper powder - 1 ½ teaspoons
- Lemon wedges - 4
- Sweet chilli sauce, to serve

Instructions:

1. Start by rinsing the calamari rings thoroughly and pat dry with paper towels.
2. Place the rings in a bowl. Pour the lemon juice over it and allow it to marinate for 30 minutes.
3. Drain the calamari rings in a colander.
4. In a shallow dish, combine flour and garlic powder.
5. Beat the egg whites and milk in a separate shallow dish.
6. In a third shallow dish, mix the panko bread crumbs, salt, and pepper.
7. Roll each ring of calamari into the flour mixture, pressing onto the rings gently to make sure they are evenly coated.
8. Take the ring out of the flour mixture and dip them into the egg mixture.
9. Finally dredge each ring on the bread crumbs mixture, making sure they are evenly coated on all sides.
10. Preheat the air fryer to 200°C (400°F).
11. Place the coated calamari rings in the air fryer basket, making sure they are not overcrowded.
12. Spray the tops with cooking oil.
13. Air fry for 4 minutes, flip the rings with a tong, then spray with oil again.
14. Continue cooking for 3 more minutes until the rings are golden brown and crispy.
15. Once cooked, remove the calamari rings from the air fryer and place them on a paper towel-lined plate to remove excess oil.
16. Serve with lemon wedges and sweet chilli sauce or your favourite dipping sauce.

Nutrition Value:

Calories: 591 | Fat: 15g | Saturates: 2g | Carbs: 87g | Sugars: 7g | Fibre: 5g | Protein: 26g | Salt: 0g

FISH AND CHIPS IN AIR FRYER

Preparation Time: 40 minutes | Cooking Time: 30 minutes | Servings: 4

Ingredients:

For chips:

- Baking potatoes - 2
- Olive oil - 2 tablespoons
- Seasoned salt - ½ teaspoon

For fish:

- Cod fillets or other white fish - 1 pound
- All-purpose flour - 120g (1 cup)
- Buttermilk - 125ml (½ cup)
- Egg - 1
- Bread crumbs -147g (1 cup)
- Lemon pepper - 2 teaspoons

Instructions:

1. Cut the potatoes into 1.5cm wedges. In a pan, boil the potatoes in water and simmer for 4 minutes. Drain the potatoes and pat dry with a paper towel.
2. Preheat the air fryer to 200°C (400°F).
3. Arrange the potatoes on the air fryer basket and cook for about 20 minutes until crisp, shaking the basket halfway through.
4. While the fries are in the air fryer, put one tablespoon of flour on a plate and season with salt and pepper to taste.
5. In a separate bowl, whisk the buttermilk and egg.
6. In another bowl, mix the bread crumbs and lemon pepper.
7. Dip the fish in the egg mixture, then in the flour mixture, ensuring it is well-coated on all sides.
8. Spray the fish with cooking oil, then place it in the air fryer basket.
9. Cook at 200°C (400°F) for 11 to 13 minutes, until cooked through and flaky.
10. Add the fries to the air fryer and cook until heated through, which usually takes about 2 minutes.

Nutrition Value:

Calories: 449 | Fat: 11g | Saturates: 2g | Carbs: 56g | Sugars: 3g | Fibre: 3g | Protein: 30g | Salt: 0.52g

AIR FRYER MAHI MAHI

Preparation Time: 5 minutes | Cooking Time: 15 minutes | Servings: 4

Ingredients:

- Mahi Mahi fillets - 4
- Grapeseed oil - 2 tablespoons
- Panko bread crumbs - 295g (2 cups)
- Bagel seasoning - 1 teaspoon
- Garlic salt - ½ teaspoon
- Ground turmeric - ½ teaspoon
- Ground black pepper - ½ teaspoon
- Cooking spray
- Fresh parsley, chopped - 1 teaspoon
- Lemon wedges - 4

Instructions:

1. Prepare the air fryer by preheating it to 200°C (400°F) for 5 minutes.
2. While the air fryer is heating, place the Mahi Mahi fillets on a platter and drizzle with grapeseed oil.
3. In a shallow dish, combine the panko bread crumbs, bagel seasoning, garlic salt, ground turmeric, and pepper.
4. Dip each Mahi Mahi fillet in the panko mixture to coat it thoroughly.
5. Arrange the fillets in a single layer in the air fryer basket, ensuring they do not overlap.
6. Spray the fillets with non-stick spray.
7. Cook the fish in the preheated air fryer for 12 to 15 minutes, flipping them halfway through. The fish should easily flake with a fork.
8. Once the fish is cooked, take it out of the air fryer.
9. Garnish with fresh chopped parsley and lemon wedges.
10. Serve right away.

Nutrition Value:

Calories: 304 | Fat: 9g | Saturates: 1g | Carbs: 41g | Sugars: 0g | Fibre: 1g | Protein: 27g | Salt: 0.67g

CRISPY SEA BASS IN AIR FRYER

Preparation Time: 15 minutes | Cooking Time: 15 minutes | Servings: 1

Ingredients:

- Sea Bass - 1
- Olive Oil - 60ml (¼ Cup)
- Kosher Salt - 1 teaspoon
- Black Pepper - ½ teaspoon
- Paprika - 1 teaspoon

- Lemon Pepper Seasoning Base - 1 teaspoon
- Garlic Powder - 1 teaspoon.
- Onion Powder - 1 teaspoon
- Parsley Flakes - 1 teaspoon.

Instructions:

1. Cut the sea bass into 4 to 5 chunks. Wash, pat dry and set aside.
2. Add all the ingredients, except the sea bass, to a bowl.
3. Mix the seasoning ingredients well.
4. Place the fish in a shallow dish.
5. Pour the seasoning mixture over the fish, and coat all sides evenly.
6. Spray the air fryer basket or tray with olive oil to prevent sticking.
7. Place the seasoned fish in the air fryer tray.
8. Set the air fryer temperature to 160°C (320°F).
9. Air fry the fish for 12 to 15 minutes.
10. Check if the fish is ready, and cook for a few more minutes if needed.
11. Remove the fish from the air fryer and serve hot.

Nutrition Value:

Calories: 545 | Fat: 8g | Saturates: 6g | Carbs: 8g | Sugars: 0g | Fibre: 2g | Protein: 8g | Salt: 0.2g

SIDE DISHES

AIR-FRIED HASSELBACK POTATOES

Preparation Time: 10 minutes | Cooking Time: 40 minutes | Servings: 4

Ingredients:

- Medium russet potatoes - 4
- Olive oil extra virgin - 4 tablespoons
- Ground black pepper - 1 teaspoon
- Kosher salt - ½ teaspoon
- Garlic powder - 1 teaspoon
- Onion powder - 1 teaspoon
- Parmesan cheese - 2 tablespoons
- Fresh parsley, chopped - 1 tablespoon

Instructions:

1. Preheat the air fryer to 180°C (360°F).
2. Prepare the air fryer basket by lining it with parchment paper or spraying it with nonstick cooking oil.
3. While the air fryer is heating up, wash and dry the potatoes.
4. Using a sharp knife, make thin slices (about ¼ inch) into the potatoes, careful not to cut all the way through.
5. Place the potatoes in a bowl and toss them with olive oil, Kosher salt, ground black pepper, onion powder, and garlic powder.
6. Arrange the potatoes in the air fryer basket, ensuring they are not overcrowded.
7. Set the timer for 20 minutes. After 20 minutes, remove the basket and gently toss the potatoes.
8. Return the potatoes to the air fryer and set the timer for an additional 15 minutes.
9. Check the potatoes after 15 minutes. They should be golden brown and crispy. If they need a little more time, add 5 minutes.
10. Once the set time elapses, remove the potatoes from the air fryer and allow them to cool for a couple of minutes.
11. Sprinkle with parmesan cheese and fresh chopped parsley on top before serving.

Nutrition Value:

Calories: 308 | Fat: 15g | Saturates: 2g | Carbs: 40g | Sugars: 1g | Fibre: 3g | Protein: 6g | Salt: 0.34g

AIR FRY CHEESY CAULIFLOWER

Preparation Time: 10 minutes | Cooking Time: 15 minutes | Servings: 4

Ingredients:

- Cauliflower - ½ head
- Olive oil - 2 tablespoons
- Garlic powder - ½ teaspoon
- Salt and pepper, to taste
- Parmesan cheese, shredded - 30g (⅓ cup)

Instructions:

1. Wash and cut the cauliflower into florets.
2. In a large bowl, toss the cauliflower with olive oil, garlic powder, salt and pepper.
3. Arrange the coated cauliflower florets in the air fryer basket.
4. Set the temperature to 200°C (400°F) and the time to 15 minutes.
5. Remove the cauliflowers once the set time elapses. The cauliflower should be tender, and the cheese golden brown and bubbly.
6. Serve immediately.

Nutrition Value:

Calories: 114 | Fat: 9g | Saturates: 2g | Carbs: 4g | Sugars: 1g | Fibre: 1g | Protein: 4g | Salt: 0.16g

APPLESAUCE IN AIR FRYER

Preparation Time: 5 minutes | Cooking Time: 20 minutes | Servings: 3

Ingredients:

- Apples - 450g (1 pound)
- Lemon juice - ½ teaspoon (optional)
- Cinnamon - 1 teaspoon
- Brown sugar - ½ teaspoon
- Water - 60ml (¼ cup)

Instructions:

1. Peel and core the apples. Cut the apples into small chunks.
2. Place a cake tin in the air fryer and preheat it to 200°C (400°F) for 3 minutes.
3. Transfer the apples to the cake tin.
4. Pour hot water over the apples until covered.
5. Add the cinnamon and brown sugar and stir to dissolve. Squeeze in lemon juice to keep the applesauce from going brown.
6. Cover the cake tin with aluminium foil and place it in the air fryer
7. Air fry the apples for 20 to 25 minutes. Stir the apples every 5 minutes. The apples are ready when they are soft and easily mashed with a fork.
8. Once the set time elapses, use a fork or potato masher to mash them into a chunky sauce.
9. Taste and adjust seasoning. If you like, you can add more sugar or cinnamon to give it a sweeter flavour.
10. The applesauce can be served warm or chilled. You can store the applesauce in the refrigerator for up to a week.

Nutrition Value:

Calories: 81 | Fat: 0g | Saturates: 0g | Carbs: 22g | Sugars: 16g | Fibre: 4g | Protein: 0g | Salt: 0g

AIR FRYER BAKED BEANS

Preparation Time: 10 minutes | Cooking Time: 20 minutes | Servings: 4

Ingredients:

- Small onion - 1
- Bacon - 4 slices
- Baked beans - 790g (28 ounces)
- Brown sugar - 28g (¼ cup)
- Ketchup - 60ml (1/4 cup)

- Yellow mustard - 1 tablespoon
- Worcestershire sauce - 1 tablespoon
- Apple cider vinegar - 1 tablespoon
- Honey - 1 tablespoon

Instructions:

1. Dice the onion and sauté it over medium heat in a nonstick frying pan. Remove and keep on a plate.
2. Dice the bacon into small pieces. Sauté it on the frying pan over medium heat.
3. Combine the onion, bacon and all the remaining ingredients (except the baked beans) in a large bowl and mix well.
4. Stir in the baked beans gently.
5. Transfer the mixture into an oven-safe casserole dish that fits comfortably into the air fryer.
6. Place the casserole dish on the air fryer basket.
7. Set the temperature to 195°C (380°F), using the air fryer setting and the timer to 20 minutes.
8. Stir frequently as the dish cooks up.
9. Once the set time elapses, remove it from the air fryer.
10. Ladle into bowls and serve with hot crusty bread.

Nutrition Value:

Calories: 437 | Fat: 18g | Saturates: 7g | Carbs: 64g | Sugars: 22g | Fibre: 11g | Protein: 11g | Salt: 1.08g

AIR-FRIED STUFFED PORTOBELLO MUSHROOMS

Preparation Time: 10 minutes | Cooking Time: 15 minutes | Servings: 4

Ingredients:

- Ground beef - 450g (1 pound)
- Onion, diced - ¼
- Garlic cloves. minced - 2
- Green pepper. diced - 1
- Tomato sauce - 500ml (2 cups)
- Olive oil - 1 tablespoon
- Portobello mushroom caps - 4
- Mozzarella cheese, shredded - 40g (⅓ cup)
- Parmesan cheese, shredded - 1 tablespoon

Instructions:

1. Sauté the ground beef, garlic, onion, and pepper in a large saucepan until tender.
2. Add the tomato sauce to the pan and simmer over low heat for 10 minutes until thick.
3. Preheat the air fryer to 180°C (360°F).
4. Clean the Portobello mushroom caps with a damp cloth and remove the gills.
5. Brush each mushroom cap with olive oil.
6. Place the mushrooms in the air fryer basket and cook them cap side up for 5 minutes.
7. Flip them over and fill the mushroom caps with the beef mixture, pressing the filling down firmly.
8. Top them off with mozzarella and parmesan cheese.
9. Air fry for 8 to 10 minutes or until the mushroom is tender and the cheese has melted.
10. Remove the mushrooms from the air fryer and let them cool for a few minutes before serving.

Nutrition Value:

Calories: 467 | Fat: 37g | Saturates: 12g | Carbs: 13g | Sugars: 8g | Fibre: 4g | Protein: 23g | Salt: 0g

AIR-FRIED CREAMY GREEN BEAN CASSEROLE

Preparation Time: 5 minutes | Cooking Time: 15 minutes | Servings: 6

Ingredients:

- Green beans - 400g (14 ounces)
- Condensed cream of mushroom soup - 400ml (14 ounces)
- Medium onion - 1

Instructions:

1. Prepare the air fryer by preheating it to 180°C (360°F)
2. Grease a baking dish that will fit comfortably in the air fryer.
3. Dice and lightly fry the onions over medium heat in a non-stick pan.
4. Take a bowl and combine the beans, condensed soup, and half of the fried onions.
5. Pour the mixture into the baking dish and top it off with the remaining onions.
6. Air fry for 15 minutes or until the onions are golden brown and the casserole is heated through.
7. Serve immediately.

Nutrition Value:

Calories: 229 | Fat: 15g | Saturates: 7g | Carbs: 19g | Sugars: 2g | Fibre: 2g | Protein: 4g | Salt: 0.6g

CORNBREAD MUFFIN IN AIR FRYER

Preparation Time: 10 minutes | Cooking Time: 15 minutes | Servings: 12

Ingredients:

- Yellow cornmeal - 100g (¾ cup)
- All-purpose flour - 120g (1 cup)
- White sugar - 1 tablespoon
- Baking powder - 1 ½ teaspoons
- Baking soda - ½ teaspoon
- Kosher salt - ¼ teaspoon
- Buttermilk - 250ml (1 cup)
- Eggs, beaten - 2
- Unsalted butter, melted - 6 tablespoons

Instructions:

1. Preheat the air fryer to 160°C (320°F).
2. Put together the cornmeal, flour, sugar, baking powder, baking soda, and salt in a large bowl. Mix the ingredients until well combined.
3. In a different bowl, mix the buttermilk and eggs. Whisk the ingredients until well combined.
4. Slowly pour the wet ingredients into the cornmeal mixture, stirring until combined. Be careful not to overmix the batter.
5. Take a muffin pan that fits into the air fryer (you can also use silicone cups) and grease it with cooking spray or butter.
6. Fill each muffin cup with the batter, filling them about 3/4 of the way.
7. Place the muffin pan in the air fryer and cook for 6 to 7 minutes. Once done, the tops should be golden brown, and a toothpick inserted into the muffin centre should come clean.
8. Carefully remove the muffin pan from the air fryer and let the muffins cool for a few minutes before serving.

Nutrition Value:

Calories: 217 | Fat: 11g | Saturates: 6g | Carbs: 25g | Sugars: 4g | Fibre: 2g | Protein: 5g | Salt: 0.18g

AIR FRYER GARLIC BUTTER CARROTS

Preparation Time: 5 minutes | Cooking Time: 8 minutes | Servings: 6

Ingredients:

- Medium carrots - 3
- Garlic cloves - 2
- Butter - 2 tablespoons
- Salt - ½ teaspoon
- Pepper - ½ teaspoon

Instructions:

1. Peel and slice the carrots into circles.
2. Melt the two tablespoons of butter in a small pan over medium heat.
3. Mince two cloves of garlic and add them to the butter.
4. Sauté the minced garlic for 1 to 2 minutes or until fragrant.
5. Place the sliced carrots in the air fryer basket and brush the garlic butter over them.
6. Air fry at 200°C (400°F) for 8 to 10 minutes.
7. Shake the basket and cook for 3 to 5 more minutes or until the carrots are tender and lightly browned.
8. Remove the basket from the air fryer and sprinkle the carrots with salt and pepper before serving.

Nutrition Value:

Calories: 97 | Fat: 8g | Saturates: 5g | Carbs:7g | Sugars: 4g | Fibre: 2g | Protein: 5g | Salt: 321mg

AIR FRYER YORKSHIRE PUDDING

Preparation Time: 5 minutes | Cooking Time: 15 minutes | Servings: 12

Ingredients:

- All-purpose flour - 120 grams (1 cup)
- Salt - ½ teaspoon
- Large eggs - 3
- Whole milk, semi-skimmed - 250ml (1 cup)
- Vegetable oil - 3 tablespoon

Instructions:

1. Sift the all-purpose flour into a large bowl and add a pinch of salt. Stir until well combined.
2. Now crack in the three eggs, splash in a little milk, and whisk them together using a balloon whisk.
3. Gradually pour in the remaining milk while stirring, until the batter becomes smooth and free of lumps.
4. Allow the batter to rest for 30 minutes or overnight in the fridge.
5. Place a silicone muffin tin in the air fryer basket and add a half teaspoon of vegetable oil to each.
6. Preheat the air fryer to 200°C (400°F) for 10 minutes.
7. Stir the batter well before pouring it into the muffin tin, filling it about halfway.
8. Cook the pudding for 10 minutes, until golden brown and puffed on top. The pudding will still be a bit doughy underneath.
9. Use tongs to turn them over and cook for an additional 5 minutes. You may need to cook up to 10 minutes for larger ones.
10. Once done, the puddings should be golden on top, crispy on the edges, and light and airy. If they still feel heavy, cook them for some more time.
11. Serve immediately with roast beef and gravy!

Nutrition Value:

Calories: 98 | Fat: 5g | Saturates: 1g | Carbs: 9g | Sugars: 1g | Fibre: 0.3g | Protein: 3g | Salt: 0.12g

BAKED SWEET POTATO IN AIR FRYER

Preparation Time: 2 minutes | Cooking Time: 40 minutes | Servings: 3

Ingredients:

- Sweet potatoes - 3
- Olive oil - 1 tablespoon
- Kosher salt - 1 teaspoon

Instructions:

1. Turn on the air fryer and set the temperature to (195°C) 380°F.
2. Take a fork and poke holes all over the surface of the sweet potatoes.
3. Rub a small amount of olive oil onto the skin of the sweet potatoes and sprinkle a pinch of salt over it.
4. Place the sweet potato in the air fryer basket, spaced apart.
5. Cook for 35 to 40 minutes or until the sweet potatoes are tender when pierced with a fork.
6. Remove the sweet potatoes from the air fryer and cut them open.
7. Place a small amount of butter on top of the sweet potato. You can also add brown sugar or any other desired toppings.
8. Serve and enjoy.

Nutrition Value:

Calories: 146 | Fat: 0.5g | Saturates: 0g | Carbs: 34g | Sugars: 1g | Fibre: 0.3g | Protein: 2.5g | Salt: 0.09g

AIR-FRIED SAVORY BEEF JERKY

Preparation Time: 30 minutes | Cooking Time: 1 hour 15 minutes | Servings: 6

Ingredients:

- Inside round steak - 450g 1 pound
- Soy sauce - 2 tablespoons
- Worcestershire sauce - 2 tablespoons
- Brown sugar - 2 teaspoons
- Table salt - 1 teaspoon
- Pepper - 1 teaspoon
- Garlic powder - 1 teaspoon
- Onion powder - 1 teaspoon
- Paprika - 1 teaspoon
- Liquid smoke - 2 tablespoons (optional)

Instructions:

1. Put the steak in the refrigerator for 30 minutes to get them firm.
2. Once they are firm, slice the steak into thin strips, about 1/4 inch thick.
3. Mix the soy sauce, Worcestershire sauce, brown sugar, salt, pepper, garlic powder, onion powder, paprika and liquid smoke (if using).
4. Place the beef strips in a large resealable bag or container and pour the marinade over the top. Make sure that each piece of beef is well-coated in the marinade.
5. Allow it to marinate for at least 1 hour or overnight in the refrigerator.
6. Take the beef out from the marinade, shaking off any excess, and transfer the strips in the air fryer.
7. Select "Dehydrate" mode on the air fryer and set the temperature to 50°C (130°F).
8. Dehydrate the meat for about 60 to 90 minutes in the air fryer or until the jerky is dry and slightly chewy. If the strips are overlapping, move them around after 30 minutes.
9. Keep it stored in an airtight container or resealable bags.

Nutrition Value:

Calories: 110 | Fat: 3g | Saturates: 1g | Carbs: 2g | Sugars: 1g | Fibre: 1g | Protein: 18g | Salt: 0.84g

AIR FRY CRISPY CHICKPEAS

Preparation Time: 3 minutes | Cooking Time: 20 minutes | Servings: 4

Ingredients:

- Chickpeas drained and rinsed - 14 ounces
- Olive oil - 1 tablespoon
- Garlic powder - ½ teaspoon
- Smoked paprika - ½ teaspoon
- Kosher salt - ½ teaspoon
- Cumin - ¼ teaspoon

Instructions:

1. Start by draining and rinsing a can of chickpeas (also known as garbanzo beans) and patting them dry with a paper towel.
2. In a small bowl, mix together the olive oil, garlic powder, smoked paprika, kosher salt, and cumin.
3. Add the chickpeas to the bowl and toss to coat them evenly in the mixture.
4. Preheat your air fryer to 200°C (400°F).
5. Once preheated, add the chickpeas to the fryer basket, spreading them out in an even layer.
6. Cook for 15 to 20 minutes, shaking the basket every 5 minutes, until the chickpeas are golden brown and crispy.
7. Once done, remove the chickpeas from the fryer and let them cool for a few minutes.
8. Enjoy the chickpeas as a snack or add them to salads, sandwiches, or other dishes.

Nutrition Value:

Calories: 196 | Fat: 6g | Saturates: 1g | Carbs: 28g | Sugars: 5g | Fibre: 8g | Protein: 9g | Salt: 0.3g

AIR FRYER CHEESE CURDS

Preparation Time: 36 minutes | Cooking Time: 4 minutes | Servings: 4

Ingredients:

- Cheese curds - 210g (8 ounces)
- All-purpose flour - 40g (⅓ cup)
- Large egg - 1
- Panko bread crumbs - 150g (1 cup)
- Garlic powder - 1 teaspoon
- Smoked paprika - ¼ teaspoon

Instructions:

1. Whisk the egg in a small bowl.
2. Mix the panko bread crumbs, garlic powder, and smoked paprika in a second bowl.
3. Toss the cheese curds with flour in a third bowl, ensuring they are coated evenly.
4. Remove the cheese curds from the flour and toss them in the egg.
5. Dip the cheese curds in the breadcrumb mixture, gently pressing to make them stick.
6. Place the cheese curds on a baking sheet and freeze them for 30 minutes.
7. Once they are frozen, generously spray the curds with cooking oil.
8. Preheat the air fryer to 200°C (400°F).
9. Place the cheese curds in the preheated air fryer basket in a single layer, ensuring not to overcrowd them.
10. Air fry for 3 to 4 minutes or until crispy and golden brown.
11. Once done, remove the cheese curds from the air fryer and place them on a plate lined with paper towels to remove excess oil.
12. Serve the cheese curds immediately while they are still warm and gooey!

Nutrition Value:

Calories: 339 | Fat: 20g | Saturates: 11g | Carbs: 19g | Sugars: 1g | Fibre: 1g | Protein: 19g | Salt: 0.5g

AIR-FRIED POTATO CHIPS

Preparation Time: 15 minutes | Cooking Time: 20 minutes | Servings: 4

Ingredients:

- Russet potatoes - 2
- Olive oil - 1 tablespoon
- Salt and seasonings, to taste

Instructions:

1. Start by washing and slicing the potatoes as thinly as possible, around ⅛ inch slices.
2. Soak the slices in cold water for about 15-30 minutes to remove the starch.
3. Drain the potatoes and dab them dry with a paper towel.
4. Preheat the air fryer to 190°C (380°F).
5. Place the potato slices in a bowl and toss them with olive oil to coat them evenly.
6. Season the slices with salt and any other desired seasonings.
7. Transfer the potato slices into the air fryer basket.
8. Cook the chips in the air fryer for about 8 to 10 minutes.
9. Shake the basket to separate the potato slices and continue cooking for 12 to 15 more minutes. Keep a close eye on the chips as they cook, as they can burn quickly.
10. Remove the chips from the air fryer and place them on a paper towel-lined plate to soak up any excess oil.
11. Serve and enjoy!

Nutrition Value:

Calories: 115 | Fat: 4g | Saturates: 1g | Carbs: 19g | Sugars: 1g | Fibre: 1g | Protein: 2g | Salt: 0.1g

KETO CHOCOLATE CHIP COOKIES IN AIR FRYER

Preparation Time: 8 minutes | Cooking Time: 6 minutes | Servings: 12

Ingredients:

- All-purpose flour - 170g (1 ¼ cups)
- Baking soda - ½ teaspoon
- Salt - ½ teaspoon
- Unsalted butter, softened - 113g (½ cup)
- Granulated sugar - 150g (¾ cup)
- Large egg - 1
- Vanilla extract - 1 teaspoon
- Chocolate chips - 170g (1 cup)

Instructions:

1. Start by preheating the air fryer to 180°C (360°F).
2. In a medium-sized mixing bowl, combine the all-purpose flour, baking soda, and salt.
3. In a separate large mixing bowl, cream together the softened butter and granulated sugar until light and fluffy.
4. Beat in the egg and vanilla extract.
5. Gradually mix in the dry ingredients from the first bowl until well combined.
6. Stir in the chocolate chips.
7. Use a spoon to scoop the dough and form cookies about 2 tablespoons in size.
8. Place the cookies in the air fryer basket, making sure to leave enough room for the cookies to expand.
9. Cook the cookies for about 8 to 10 minutes or until golden brown and set.
10. Take the cookies out of the air fryer basket and let them cool.
11. Serve and enjoy your warm and delicious air-fried chocolate chip cookies!

Nutrition Value:

Calories: 140 | Fat: 12g | Saturates: 8g | Carbs: 6g | Sugars: 1g | Fibre: 2g | Protein: 2g | Salt: 0.1g

APPLE CINNAMON CHIPS IN AIR FRYER

Preparation Time: 5 minutes | Cooking Time: 8 minutes | Servings: 2

Ingredients:

- Apple - 1
- Sugar - 1 tablespoon
- Ground cinnamon - ½ teaspoon
- Ground cardamom - 1 pinch
- Ground ginger - 1 pinch
- Salt - 1 pinch

Instructions:

1. Preheat the air fryer to 180°C (360°F).
2. Core and peel the apple. Thinly slice it into circles.
3. In a medium-sized mixing bowl, toss the apple slices with sugar, cinnamon, cardamom, ginger and salt until they are coated evenly.
4. Place the apple slices in the air fryer basket in a single layer, making sure not to overcrowd the basket.
5. Cook the apple slices for about 8 minutes or until they are crispy and golden brown.
6. Remove the apple chips from the air fryer.
7. Serve and enjoy your delicious snack!

Nutrition Value:

Calories: 72 | Fat: 1g | Saturates: 1g | Carbs: 19g | Sugars: 15g | Fibre: 2g | Protein: 1g | Salt: 1mg

BANANA MUFFINS IN AIR FRYER

Preparation Time: 10 minutes | Cooking Time: 10 minutes | Servings: 12

Ingredients:

- All-purpose flour - 180g (1 ½ cups)
- White sugar - 150g (¾ cup)
- Baking powder - 1 teaspoon
- Baking soda - 1 teaspoon
- Cinnamon - 1 tsp
- Salt - ½ teaspoon
- Large bananas - 3
- Egg - 1
- Butter, melted - 76g (⅓ cup)

Instructions:

1. Whisk together the flour, baking powder, baking soda, cinnamon and salt in a large mixing bowl.
2. In a separate bowl, beat the sugar, melted butter, and eggs until well combined.
3. Stir in the mashed bananas and mix until combined.
4. Slowly fold the dry ingredients into the wet ingredients until just combined. Do not overmix.
5. Grease the muffin cups of your air fryer (or use muffin liners) and fill each cup about ⅔ full with the batter.
6. Set the air fryer to 180°C (360°F and bake for 12 to 15 minutes or until a toothpick inserted into the centre comes clean.
7. Let the muffins cool in the air fryer for a few minutes before removing them from the cups and serving.

Nutrition Value:

Calories: 183 | Fat: 6g | Saturates: 3g | Carbs: 31g | Sugars: 16g | Fibre: 1g | Protein: 2g | Salt: 0.24g

BACON CRACKERS IN AIR FRYER

Preparation Time: 5 minutes | Cooking Time: 5 minutes | Servings: 2

Ingredients:

- Flax seed or multigrain crackers - 8
- Bacon - 4 strips
- Brown sugar - 2 tablespoons

Instructions:

1. Prepare the air fryer by preheating it to 200°C (400°F).
2. Cut the bacon strips into slightly larger sizes than the cracker size.
3. Place the bacon in the air fryer basket and cook for 4 minutes.
4. Place the crackers in the air fryer basket, stack the bacon on top, and sprinkle with brown sugar.
5. Cook for 1 to 2 minutes or until golden brown. Enjoy!

Nutrition Value:

Calories: 242 | Fat: 16g | Saturates: 5g | Carbs: 20g | Sugars: 13g | Fibre: 1g | Protein: 5g | Salt: 0.33g

LOW-CARB GREEN TOMATOES IN AIR FRYER

Preparation Time: 15 minutes | Cooking Time: 10 minutes | Servings: 4

Ingredients:

- Pork rinds, finely crushed - 34g (1 cup)
- Green tomatoes - 3
- Egg whisked - 1
- Honey mustard - 1 tablespoon
- Whipping cream - 2 tablespoons
- ThinSlim bread toasted - 1 slice
- Slap Yo Mamma - 1 tablespoon
- EVOO spray

Instructions:

1. Prepare the air fryer by preheating it to 200°C (400°F).
2. Take a large bowl and mix the crushed pork rinds, bread crumbs, and seasoning.
3. Blend the egg, whipping cream, and honey mustard in another bowl.
4. Cut the green tomatoes into ½-inch thick slices.
5. Dip each tomato slice in the egg mixture, then into the pork rind mixture to coat thoroughly.
6. Place the coated tomato slices in a single layer on the air fryer pan and spray with EVOO.
7. Air fry for 10 minutes, flipping halfway through. Cook until desired tenderness is achieved.
8. Remove the tomatoes from the air fryer and set them aside to cool down before serving.

Nutrition Value:

Calories: 123 | Fat: 7g | Saturates: 3g | Carbs: 8g | Sugars: 5g | Fibre: 2g | Protein: 8g | Salt: 0.22g

DESSERTS

PERFECT BAKED APPLES IN AIR FRYER

Preparation Time: 10 minutes | Cooking Time: 25 minutes | Servings: 4

Ingredients:

- Medium apples - 2
- White sugar - 2 teaspoons

- Melted butter - 1 tablespoon
- Cinnamon - ½ teaspoon

For topping

- Rolled oats - 78g (½ cup)
- Brown sugar - 50g (¼ cup)
- Chopped pecans - 37g (¼ cup)

- Ground cinnamon -1 teaspoon
- Butter - 57g (¼ cup)

Instructions:

1. Start by preheating your air fryer to 175°C (350°F).
2. Slice the apples in half from top to bottom and scoop out the core and seeds with a spoon, creating a hollow shell.
3. Using a pastry brush or spoon, evenly spread melted butter over the cut surface of the apples.
4. Add the sugar and cinnamon to a small mixing bowl, and stir to combine. Sprinkle the mixture generously over the apples.
5. Place the apples in the air fryer basket and cook for 10 to 12 minutes.
6. While the apples are cooking, in another small bowl, blend the topping ingredients and mix until well combined.
7. After 10 to 12 minutes, open the air fryer and add the topping mixture over the apples, spreading it evenly.
8. Close the air fryer and continue cooking for another 5 to 6 minutes or until the topping is golden brown and the apples are tender.
9. Once done, remove the apples from the air fryer and serve warm with a scoop of your favourite ice cream for an added treat.

Nutrition Value:

Calories: 253 | Fat: 6g | Saturates: 1g | Carbs: 48g | Sugars: 38g | Fibre: 7g | Protein: 3g | Salt: 0.02g

EASY S'MORES IN AIR FRYER

Preparation Time: 5 minutes | Cooking Time: 4 minutes | Servings: 9

Ingredients:

- Graham crackers - 9
- Marshmallows - 9

- Hershey chocolate bars, broken into thirds - 3

Instructions:

1. Prepare the air fryer by preheating it to 180°C (360°F).
2. Take the graham crackers and break them in half to get two squares from each cracker. Place half of the graham cracker squares in the air fryer, and set the other half aside to use as the tops of the s'mores.
3. Cut the marshmallows in half to get two thinner pieces. Place the marshmallows, cut side down, on top of the graham cracker squares in the air fryer.
4. Cook the graham crackers and marshmallows in the air fryer for 4 minutes. Keep an eye on them to ensure they won't burn.
5. Carefully remove the graham crackers and marshmallows from the air fryer using tongs. Drop a chocolate square on top of each marshmallow.
6. Place the remaining graham cracker squares on top of the chocolate to complete the s'mores.
7. Let them cool for a minute or two before enjoying your warm and gooey air fryer s'mores!

Nutrition Value:

Calories: 129 | Fat: 5g | Saturates: 2g | Carbs: 22g | Sugars: 12g | Fibre: 1g | Protein: 1g | Salt: 0.1g

AIR-FRIED PEACH GALETTE WITH CROISSANT

Preparation Time: 10 minutes | Cooking Time: 10 minutes | Servings: 4

Ingredients:

- Peaches, diced - 84g (½ cup)
- Honey - ½ teaspoon
- Cinnamon - ¼ teaspoon
- Brown sugar - 1 tablespoon
- 4 count roll of croissant - 1

Instructions:

1. Start by preheating your air fryer to 180°C (360°F).
2. Mix peaches, honey, and cinnamon in a large bowl until well combined.
3. Take the crescents and pull them apart into individual triangles. Arrange them in a star pattern with the triangles overlapping in the centre. Press the edges together to seal them.
4. Place the crescent roll star in the air fryer basket. Sprinkle brown sugar in the centre of the star.
5. Spoon the peach mixture on top of the brown sugar.
6. Use the star-shaped ends of the crescent roll triangles to cover the edges of the peach mixture, pressing to seal the edges. Repeat this process until the entire galette is sealed.
7. Carefully place the uncooked peach galette on the air fryer tray.
8. Cook in the air fryer for 10 to 11 minutes or until the dough is golden brown and cooked.
9. Once done, remove it from the air fryer and let it cool for a few minutes before slicing and serving. Enjoy your peach galette!

Nutrition Value:

Calories: 80 | Fat: 3g | Saturates: 2g | Carbs: 12g | Sugars: 7g | Fibre: 1g | Protein: 1g | Salt: 0.06g

RASPBERRY COMPOTE CHEESECAKE IN AIR FRYER

Preparation Time: 10 minutes | Cooking Time: 10 minutes | Servings: 2

Ingredients:

- Cream cheese - 226g (8 ounces)
- Eggs - 2
- Sugar - ¾ cup

For the raspberry compote:

- Raspberries, fresh or frozen - 150g (1 ¼ cup)
- Sugar - 50g (¼ cup)

- Vanilla - ½ teaspoon
- Sour cream - 2 tablespoons

- Water - 2 tablespoons
- 1 tablespoon cornstarch, plus 1 tablespoon of water

Instructions:

1. Preheat the air fryer to 180°C (360°F) on the BAKE setting.
2. In a mixing bowl, combine the eggs, sugar and vanilla.
3. Next, add the sour cream and cream cheese to the egg mixture. Beat the ingredients together until they are smooth.
4. Pour the mixture into a ramekin.
5. Place the ramekin in a pan filled with water up to a half-inch high.
6. Place the pan in the preheated air fryer and bake for 7 minutes.
7. After 7 minutes, remove the pan and check the cheesecake. It should be slightly brown on top and firm to the touch. If not, put it back in the air fryer for a few more minutes.
8. Once the cheesecake is ready, take it out of the air fryer and allow it to cool.
9. For the raspberry compote, mix the raspberries, sugar and two tablespoons of water in a pan. Bring the mixture to a boil and use a spoon to mash the raspberries.
10. In a separate bowl, mix cornstarch and water to create a slurry.
11. Pour the cornstarch mixture into the boiling raspberry mixture and simmer for 5 minutes or until the sauce thickens.
12. Serve the cheesecake with raspberry compote on top.

Nutrition Value:

Calories: 918 | Fat: 46g | Saturates: 25g | Carbs: 118g | Sugars: 107g | Fibre: 5g | Protein: 13g | Salt: 0.44g

MINI LEMON TARTS IN AIR FRYER

Preparation Time: 5 minutes | Cooking Time: 15 minutes | Servings: 12

Ingredients:

- Mini tart shells - 12
- Lemon dessert mix - 1 box
- Raspberries, for garnishing

Instructions:

1. Begin by preheating the air fryer to 180°C (360°F) on the BAKE setting.
2. While the air fryer is preheating, place the tart shells in the air fryer basket.
3. Cook the tart shells for 1 to 2 minutes or until they are lightly golden brown and crispy.
4. While the tart shells are cooking, prepare the dessert mix according to the instructions on the box.
5. Once the filling is ready, fill the cooled tart shells with the mixture.
6. Place the stuffed tarts back in the air fryer and bake for 5 minutes.
7. Remove the mini lemon tarts from the air fryer and allow them to cool completely before serving.

Nutrition Value:

Calories: 67 | Fat: 4g | Saturates: 2g | Carbs: 6g | Sugars: 1g | Fibre: 1g | Protein: 1g | Salt: 0.04g

AIR FRYER BLUEBERRY COOKIES

Preparation Time: 10 minutes | Cooking Time: 10 minutes | Servings: 12

Ingredients:

- All-purpose flour - 120g (1 cup)
- Baking powder - ½ teaspoon
- Salt - ⅛ teaspoon
- Vegan butter, softened - 76g (⅓ cup)
- Sugar - 67g (⅓ cup) + 1 tablespoon
- Frozen blueberries - 63g (⅓ cup)
- White chocolate chips or shavings - 56g (½ cup)

Instructions:

1. Whisk the flour, baking powder, and salt in a small mixing bowl. Set the mixture aside.
2. Place the blueberries in a microwave-safe dish and thaw them for about 1 minute or until they are soft and jam-like. Let the blueberries cool.
3. Take a separate mixing bowl and cream the butter and sugar until the mixture is light and fluffy.
4. Add the thawed blueberries to the butter and sugar mixture and blend on high until they are well combined.
5. Gradually add the dry ingredients from the first step into the blueberry mixture.
6. Mix in the white chocolate chips.
7. Place the dough in the freezer for about 30 minutes to chill.
8. Preheat an air fryer to 190°C (375°F) on the BAKE setting.
9. Shape the dough into 12 equal-sized balls and place them in the air fryer basket.
10. Bake the cookies for 10 minutes and repeat the process with any remaining dough.
11. Once the cookies are ready, let them cool before serving and enjoy!

Nutrition Value:

Calories: 139 | Fat: 7g | Saturates: 3g | Carbs: 19g | Sugars: 10g | Fibre: 1g | Protein: 2g | Salt: 0.07g

FRIED OREOS IN AIR FRYER

Preparation Time: 12 minutes | Cooking Time: 5 minutes | Servings: 8

Ingredients:

- 8 Oreos
- Crescent rolls - 1 package

Instructions:

1. Start by preheating your air fryer to 180°C (360°F).
2. Remove the crescent rolls and unroll them. Use your fingers to pinch the seams together to create one large sheet of dough.
3. Use a pizza cutter or sharp knife to cut the dough into squares.
4. Take an Oreo cookie and place it in the centre of each square of dough.
5. Bring the corners of the dough up and around the Oreo, making sure to seal the seams.
6. Once all the Oreos are wrapped in dough, place them in the air fryer basket, making sure they are not touching each other.
7. Cook the wrapped Oreos in the air fryer for 5 minutes or until the dough is golden brown and crispy.
8. Remove the Oreos from the air fryer.
9. Allow the Oreos to cool for a few minutes before serving. They are best served warm and can be enjoyed with a side of vanilla ice cream or chocolate sauce.

Nutrition Value:

Calories: 155 | Fat: 8g | Saturates: 3g | Carbs: 20g | Sugars: 8g | Fibre: 1g | Protein: 2g | Salt: 0.28g

STRAWBERRY TURNOVERS IN AIR FRYER

Preparation Time: 8 minutes | Cooking Time: 10 minutes | Servings: 6

Ingredients:

- Strawberry pie filling - 1 can
- Puff pastry - 1
- Icing - 25g (¼ cup)
- Cooking spray

Instructions:

1. Begin by preheating your air fryer to 180°C (360°F).
2. Cut the puff pastry into four equal squares.
3. Take a large spoonful of strawberry filling and place it on the corner of each square.
4. Fold each square into a triangle shape, and press the edges together with a fork to seal the seams.
5. Lightly spray the top of each pastry with cooking spray.
6. Carefully place the strawberry turnovers in the air fryer basket, ensuring they do not touch each other.
7. Cook them in the air fryer for 10 minutes or until they are flaky and golden brown.
8. Once done, remove them from the air fryer and place them on a plate.
9. Allow the strawberry turnovers to cool for a few minutes before serving. You can enjoy it with a drizzle of chocolate sauce on top.

Nutrition Value:

Calories: 265 | Fat: 17g | Saturates: 4g | Carbs: 25g | Sugars: 6g | Fibre: 1g | Protein: 3g | Salt: 0.12g

APPLE HAND PIES IN AIR FRYER

Preparation Time: 8 minutes | Cooking Time: 10 minutes | Servings: 6

Ingredients:

For the crust:

- All-purpose flour - 313g (2 ½ cups)
- Shortening - 60g (¼ cup)
- Butter - 150g (⅔ cups)
- Cold water - 8 tablespoons

For the filling:

- Apple, diced - 120g (1 cup)
- Lemon juice - 1 teaspoon
- Brown sugar - 50g (¼ cup)
- Cinnamon - ½ teaspoon
- All-purpose flour - 1 tablespoon
- Oil - 3 tablespoon

Instructions:

1. Mix the flour and shortening until the shortening is fully incorporated into the flour.
2. Add butter to the flour mixture and pinch until it resembles coarse sand.
3. Gradually add cold water to the mixture.
4. Gently form the pastry into a cohesive mass.
5. Wrap the dough in plastic wrap and place it in the refrigerator for 30 minutes.
6. Remove the dough from the refrigerator.
7. Roll out the dough and cut out small circles with a bowl or cookie cutter.
8. Preheat the air fryer to 180°C (360°F) on the BAKE setting.
9. Combine all the filling ingredients and mix well until well combined.
10. Scoop around two tablespoons of the filling mixture in the centre of each dough circle.
11. Lightly brush some water on the edges of the dough circles. Fold the dough circles in half and seal the edges to create a half-moon shape.
12. Make small vents on the top of each pie with a fork and brush the tops with oil.
13. Transfer the hand pies to the air fryer basket, ensuring they are not touching each other.
14. Cook the hand pies for 5 minutes or until the crust is golden brown and flaky.
15. Once done, remove the hand pies from the air fryer and place them on a plate to cool before serving.

Nutrition Value:

Calories: 279 | Fat: 18g | Saturates: 8g | Carbs: 26g | Sugars: 6g | Fibre: 1g | Protein: 3g | Salt: 92mg

CONCLUSION

Overall, an air fryer offers a healthy way to cook a wide variety of foods. Although this machine can be a little expensive the long-term health benefits are vast and priceless. Nonetheless, it's still important to incorporate fresh foods and fruits in order to ensure you have a balanced diet. Also, remember to engage in some physical activity in your routines to stay fit.

An air fryer has shown that you can enjoy fried foods without altering the flavour and taste while still keeping your bills down. Air frying can greatly help anyone who wishes to control their weight as well as minimize the risk of lifestyle illnesses such as stroke and heart attacks. Most lifestyle diseases are associated with poor diets such as intake of large amounts of unhealthy fats. Air frying calls for zero or just little addition of cooking oils and hence, the amount of fat intake is kept at low levels. In addition, air frying eliminates some harmful compounds such as acrylamides which are associated with cancers. These harmful compounds are usually produced when cooking foods in hot oil.

Other benefits of air fryers include time-saving, less power consumption, easier clean-ups and convenience. You can cook a large number of things with this device such as roasted chicken and French fries. However, some dishes such as cereals, pasta, and cheese may not work well. For instant, pasta and rice require rehydration in boiling water to cook properly and therefore, are not suitable for an air fryer. The air fryer uses hot air to cook solid foods without the need for any liquid like water. Lastly, I'd like to thank you for reading this book, and remember to share it with your friends so that they can also enjoy the magic results of the air fryer.

Printed in Great Britain
by Amazon

30929066R00057